MathFlare

Name: ________________________

Class: __________

Teacher: ________________________

Introduction

As parents and educators, we recognize the pivotal role mathematics plays in shaping a child's academic journey and future success. Yet, the path to mathematical proficiency can often seem daunting, fraught with challenges and complexities. That's where the transformative power of MathFlare Workbooks shine through, illuminating the way forward with clarity, precision, and purpose.

Introducing MathFlare Workbooks – a beacon of guidance, a testament to excellence, and a catalyst for achievement. Crafted with meticulous care and expertise, MathFlare Workbooks stand as paragons of educational excellence, designed to nurture young minds, ignite a passion for learning, and develop a deep-rooted understanding of mathematical concepts.

Picture this: your child eagerly delves into the pages of Mathflare Workbook, greeted by a step-by-step guide illuminated with vivid examples that demystify complex mathematical concepts. With each turn of the page, they embark on a journey of discovery, encountering thoughtfully curated practice questions that reinforce learning and hone problem-solving skills. And when they unveil the answers to those very questions, a sense of accomplishment blossoms within them – a tangible reward for their hard work and dedication.

But MathFlare Workbooks are more than just tools for learning; they are pathways to comprehension, fostering a deep-seated understanding of mathematical concepts through a sequential, logical flow. From fundamental principles to advanced problem-solving strategies, every chapter builds upon the last, ensuring a robust foundation upon which future knowledge can be constructed.

As parents, we yearn for nothing more than to see our children thrive, to witness the spark of inspiration ignited within them as they conquer academic challenges with confidence and poise. MathFlare Workbooks serve as partners in this noble endeavor, offering not just practice questions, but the keys to unlocking a world of opportunity.

And for teachers, MathFlare Workbooks stand as invaluable allies in the quest to cultivate mathematical proficiency in the classroom. With answers readily available, instructors can focus on guiding and nurturing their students, confident in the knowledge that MathFlare Workbooks provide a solid framework upon which to build.

In the pages of MathFlare Workbooks, we find not just the promise of academic excellence, but the seeds of a brighter tomorrow. So let us embrace the power of mathematics, let us champion the journey of learning, and let us pave the way for a generation of young minds poised to shape the world. With MathFlare Workbooks as our guide, the possibilities are infinite, and the future, bright.

Table of Contents

MathFlare
Grade 2
MATH WORKBOOK
Step by Step Guide and Essential Practice with Answers
Addition Subtraction
Multiplication
Place Value and Expanded Notations
Geometry
MathFlare Publishing

MathFlare
Grade 2-3
MATH WORKBOOK
Step by Step Guide and Essential Practice with Answers
Addition Subtraction
Multiplication and Division
Place Value and Expanded Notations
Geometry
MathFlare Publishing

MathFlare
Grade 3
MATH WORKBOOK
Step by Step Guide and Essential Practice with Answers
Multiplication and Division
Decimals
Place Value and Expanded Notations
Fractions and Geometry
MathFlare Publishing

MathFlare
Grade 1
MATH WORKBOOK
Step by Step Guide and Essential Practice with Answers
Counting and Numbers
Addition and Subtraction
Place Value and Expanded Notations
Understanding Time
MathFlare Publishing

MathFlare
Grade 1-2
MATH WORKBOOK
Step by Step Guide and Essential Practice with Answers
Counting and Numbers
Addition and Subtraction
Place Value and Expanded Notations
Understanding Time
MathFlare Publishing

MathFlare
Grade 3-4
MATH WORKBOOK
Step by Step Guide and Essential Practice with Answers
Addition Subtraction
Multiplication Division
Place Value and Expanded Notations
Fractions and Geometry
MathFlare Publishing

MathFlare
Grade 4
MATH WORKBOOK
Step by Step Guide and Essential Practice with Answers
Addition Subtraction
Multiplication Division
Place Value and Expanded Notations
Fractions and Geometry
MathFlare Publishing

MathFlare
Grade 4-5
MATH WORKBOOK
Step by Step Guide and Essential Practice with Answers
Multiplication Division
Place Value and Expanded Notations
Fractions and Geometry
Unit Conversion
MathFlare Publishing

MathFlare
MATH
WORKBOOK
5
Step by Step Guide
and Essential Practice
with Answers
Multiplication
Division
Place Value and
Expanded
Notations
Fractions
and Geometry
Unit
Conversion
MathFlare Publishing

MathFlare
MATH
WORKBOOK
5-6
Step by Step Guide
and Essential Practice
with Answers
Multiplication
Division
Place Value and
Expanded
Notations
Fractions
and Geometry
Units and
Statistics
MathFlare Publishing

MathFlare
MATH
WORKBOOK
6
Step by Step Guide
and Essential Practice
with Answers
Integers and
Statistics
Arithmetic and
Pre-Algebra
Fractions
and Geometry
Ratio and
Percentage
MathFlare Publishing

MathFlare
MATH
WORKBOOK
6-7
Step by Step Guide
and Essential Practice
with Answers
Arithmetic and
Pre-Algebra
Ratio, Percent
Proportion
Geometry
Statistics
MathFlare Publishing

MathFlare
MATH
WORKBOOK
7
Step by Step Guide
and Essential Practice
with Answers
Pre-Algebra
Ratio, Percent
Proportion
Geometry
Statistics
MathFlare Publishing

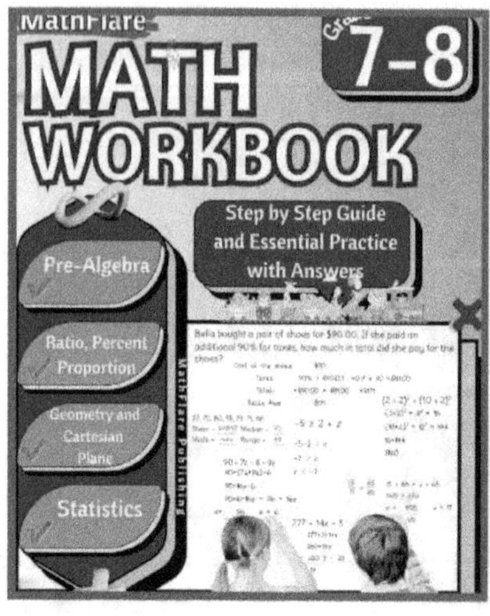
MathFlare
MATH
WORKBOOK
7-8
Step by Step Guide
and Essential Practice
with Answers
Pre-Algebra
Ratio, Percent
Proportion
Geometry and
Cartesian
Plane
Statistics
MathFlare Publishing

MathFlare
MATH
WORKBOOK
8-9
Step by Step Guide
and Essential Practice
with Answers
Pre-Algebra
Ratio, Proportion
and Percentage
Linear
Equations
Geometry and
Cartesian Plane
MathFlare Publishing

MathFlare
MATH
WORKBOOK
8
Step by Step Guide
and Essential Practice
with Answers
Pre-Algebra
Percentage
Linear
Equations
Geometry
MathFlare Publishing

Decimals

Adding Decimals

Adding decimals is like adding whole numbers, but we must align the decimal points carefully. For instance, when adding 49.88 and 45.78:

Step 1: Align the decimal points.

$$49.88$$
$$+\ 45.78$$

Step 2: Start adding from the rightmost digit (the ones place) and move to the left.
Add 8 and 8: 8 + 8 = 16. Write down 6 in the ones place and carry over 1 to the tenths place.

$$49.88$$
$$+\ 45.78$$
$$6$$

Step 3: Add the tenths place.
Add 1 (carried over from the previous step), 8, and 7: 1 + 8 + 7 = 16. Write down 6 in the tenths place and carry over 1 to the hundredths place.

$$49.88$$
$$+\ 45.78$$
$$66$$

Step 4: Continue adding digits to the left until you reach the leftmost digit:

$$49.88$$
$$+\ 45.78$$
$$9566$$

<u>Step 5: Finally, write the sum with the decimal point directly below the decimal points in the original numbers.</u>

$$
\begin{array}{r}
49.88 \\
+\ 45.78 \\
\hline
95.66
\end{array}
$$

Subtracting Decimals

Subtracting decimals follows a process like adding decimals, except instead of adding the numbers, we subtract them.

Let's solve more problems:

$$
\begin{array}{r}
10.26 \\
+\ 80.45 \\
\hline
90.71
\end{array}
\qquad
\begin{array}{r}
87.11 \\
-\ 11.31 \\
\hline
75.80
\end{array}
$$

Fractions

Fractions represent parts of a whole. They consist of a numerator (the number on top) and a denominator (the number on the bottom).

For example:

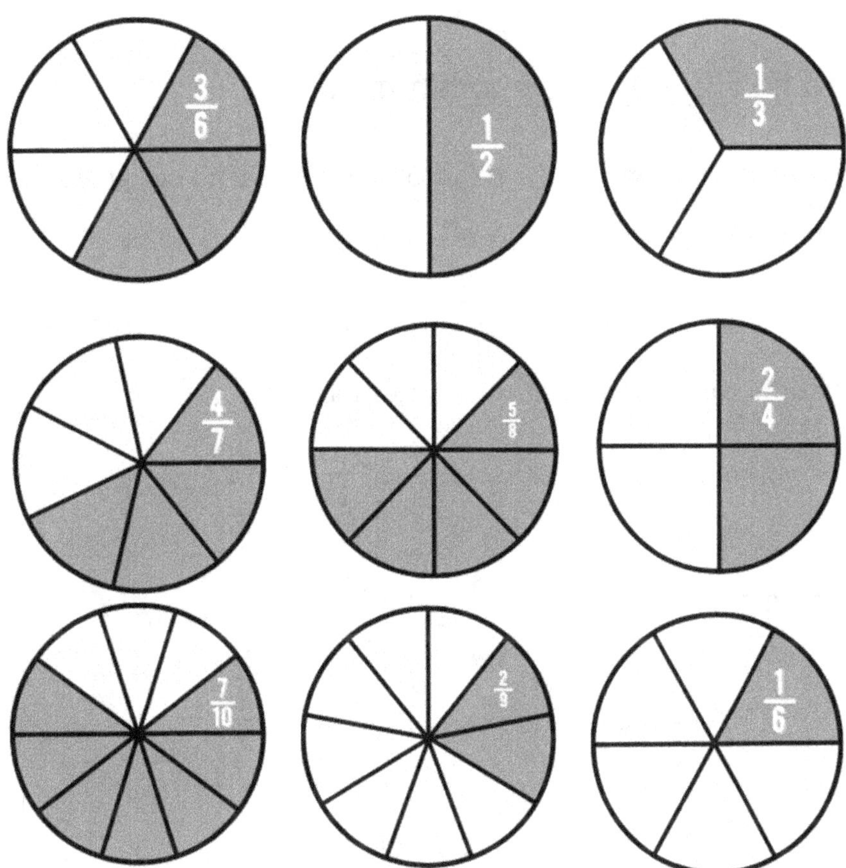

Comparing Fractions

When comparing fractions, we consider the size of their denominators. Generally, the larger the denominator, the smaller the fraction.

For example:

$\frac{1}{3}$ is smaller than $\frac{1}{2}$ because the denominator 3 is larger than the denominator 2.

If the denominators are the same, we can compare the numerators to determine which fraction is larger.

Let's solve a problem:

$$\frac{56}{60} \underset{\underline{\quad}}{<} \frac{57}{60}$$

Fractions Addition (Common Denominator)

To add fractions with a common denominator, we add their numerators together and keep the denominator the same.

For example: if we want to add $\frac{3}{5}$ and $\frac{2}{5}$ both fractions have the same denominator of 5. Therefore, to add them, we simply add their numerators:

$$\frac{3}{5} + \frac{2}{5} = \frac{3+2}{5} = \frac{5}{5}$$

Let's solve a problem:

$$\frac{1}{9} + \frac{7}{9} = \frac{1+7}{9} = \frac{8}{9}$$

Fractions Subtraction (Common Denominator)

To subtract fractions with a common denominator, we find the difference between their numerators and keep the denominator the same.

For example:

$$\frac{3}{5} - \frac{2}{5} = \frac{3-2}{5} = \frac{1}{5}$$

Let's solve a problem:

$$\frac{5}{8} - \frac{2}{8} = \frac{5-2}{8} = \frac{3}{8}$$

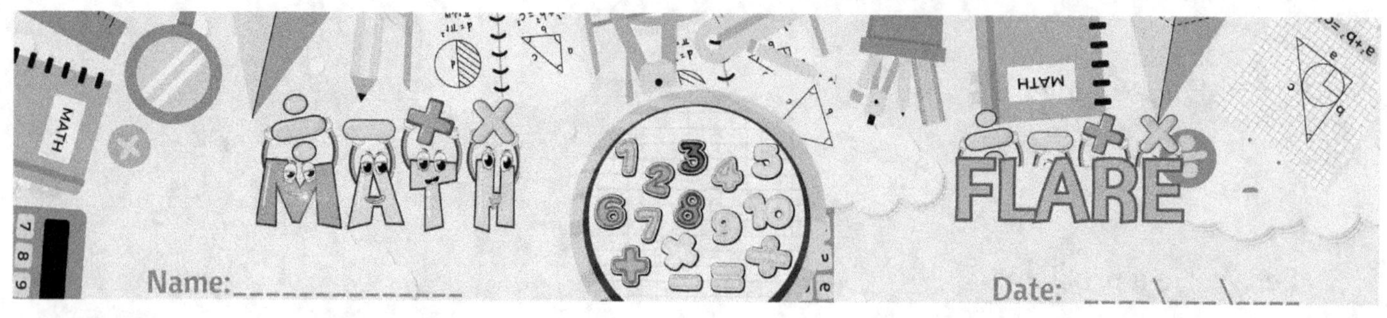

Adding Decimals

Find the sum.

1. 92.04
  + 77.03

2. 20.10
  + 94.34

3. 99.41
  + 86.85

4. 96.99
  + 85.40

5. 66.47
  + 74.35

6. 40.89
  + 39.07

7. 27.34
  + 10.24

8. 24.56
  + 77.98

9. 76.54
  + 86.39

10. 65.19
  + 29.05

11. 21.76
  + 10.05

12. 27.75
  + 90.04

13. 35.28
  + 49.78

14. 46.95
  + 29.70

15. 42.61
  + 82.21

16. 18.55
  + 95.73

17. 50.19
  + 18.81

18. 25.78
  + 33.80

19. 40.53
  + 28.68

20. 69.51
  + 53.86

Name: _______________   Date: _______________

21. 92.92 + 70.71	22. 39.57 + 57.64	23. 75.21 + 74.52	24. 66.59 + 83.97
25. 50.60 + 50.81	26. 14.53 + 15.92	27. 99.82 + 47.79	28. 96.19 + 91.99
29. 59.27 + 30.04	30. 69.06 + 59.63	31. 49.90 + 77.29	32. 52.79 + 84.25
33. 65.80 + 45.14	34. 88.87 + 18.53	35. 84.46 + 90.75	36. 47.45 + 57.86
37. 26.88 + 21.33	38. 36.13 + 51.04	39. 70.47 + 70.11	40. 24.84 + 60.75

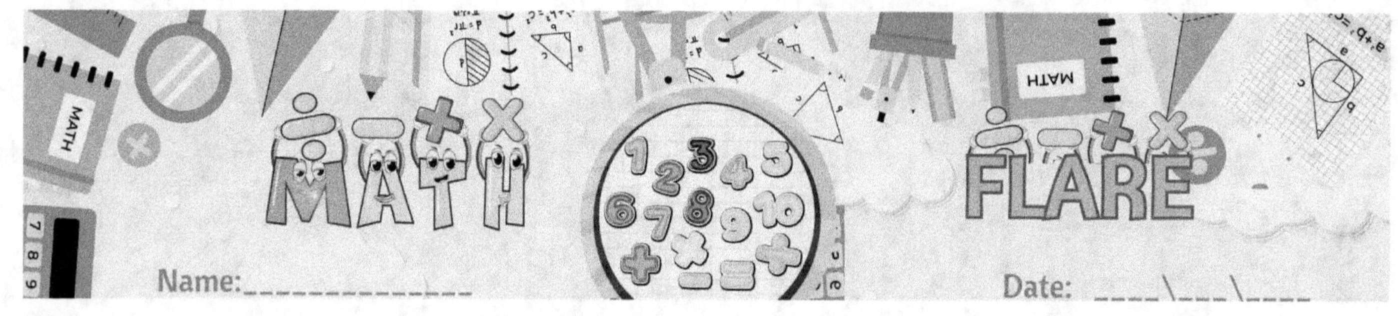

41. 83.18 + 62.97	42. 79.10 + 91.79	43. 77.68 + 12.63	44. 95.91 + 12.40
45. 22.61 + 33.78	46. 74.52 + 20.48	47. 59.61 + 19.88	48. 13.96 + 25.63
49. 27.92 + 55.31	50. 91.83 + 40.06	51. 85.65 + 58.05	52. 99.50 + 59.84
53. 13.36 + 56.66	54. 89.02 + 88.48	55. 21.66 + 55.15	56. 31.52 + 89.15
57. 15.20 + 18.31	58. 76.44 + 86.92	59. 98.18 + 60.99	60. 16.57 + 63.17

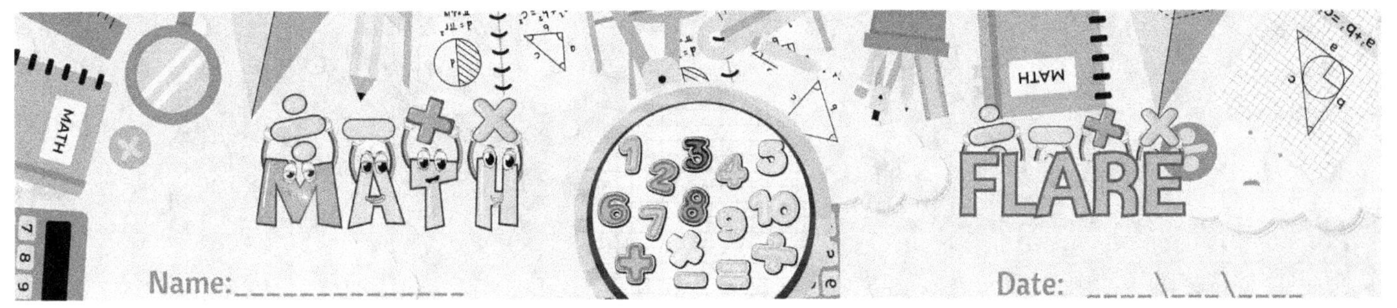

Name:________________   Date: _______________

61. 49.23 + 86.47	62. 95.91 + 60.68	63. 26.23 + 36.97	64. 98.24 + 17.01
65. 17.38 + 20.50	66. 33.12 + 25.15	67. 78.27 + 84.77	68. 75.09 + 35.13
69. 63.46 + 29.26	70. 88.43 + 31.02	71. 23.60 + 17.43	72. 90.73 + 67.46
73. 12.26 + 85.36	74. 15.28 + 51.30	75. 43.43 + 27.03	76. 27.44 + 66.92
77. 48.74 + 38.66	78. 90.83 + 99.17	79. 62.13 + 48.82	80. 43.61 + 76.38

81. 58.41 + 82.01	82. 81.11 + 11.16	83. 32.03 + 16.37	84. 20.88 + 30.43
85. 43.21 + 51.30	86. 33.45 + 78.92	87. 72.55 + 85.54	88. 49.57 + 41.80
89. 95.73 + 38.45	90. 58.42 + 40.86	91. 31.69 + 56.94	92. 73.57 + 90.34
93. 93.05 + 66.19	94. 76.40 + 49.62	95. 93.93 + 75.92	96. 72.99 + 24.64
97. 85.64 + 22.05	98. 72.60 + 41.58	99. 36.31 + 89.57	100. 45.42 + 95.88

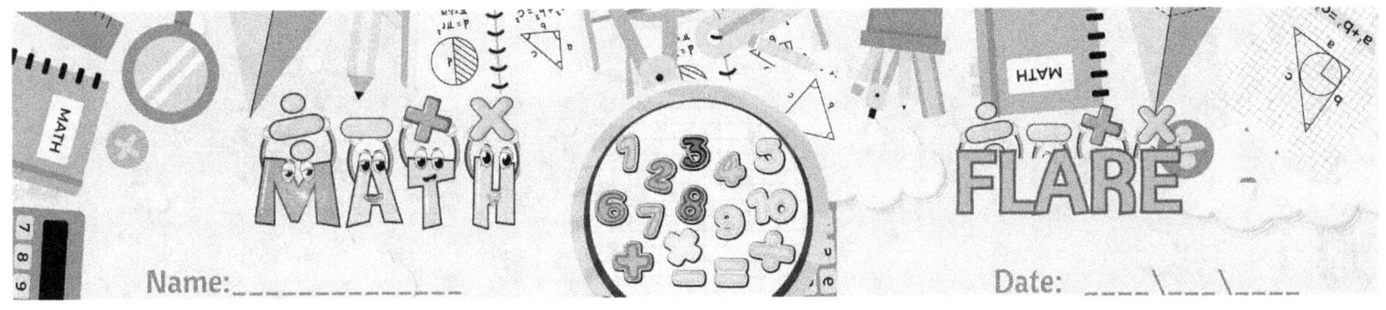

Subtracting Decimals

Find the difference.

101. 51.54 − 27.91	102. 85.55 − 49.17	103. 92.49 − 66.78	104. 96.25 − 83.58
105. 72.58 − 27.20	106. 53.81 − 41.31	107. 73.85 − 43.62	108. 28.40 − 16.77
109. 70.64 − 31.69	110. 87.22 − 74.47	111. 83.15 − 17.78	112. 65.14 − 63.28
113. 63.67 − 29.50	114. 95.35 − 61.18	115. 66.58 − 36.38	116. 64.48 − 22.00
117. 70.99 − 17.11	118. 65.17 − 17.57	119. 89.30 − 83.78	120. 33.04 − 20.57

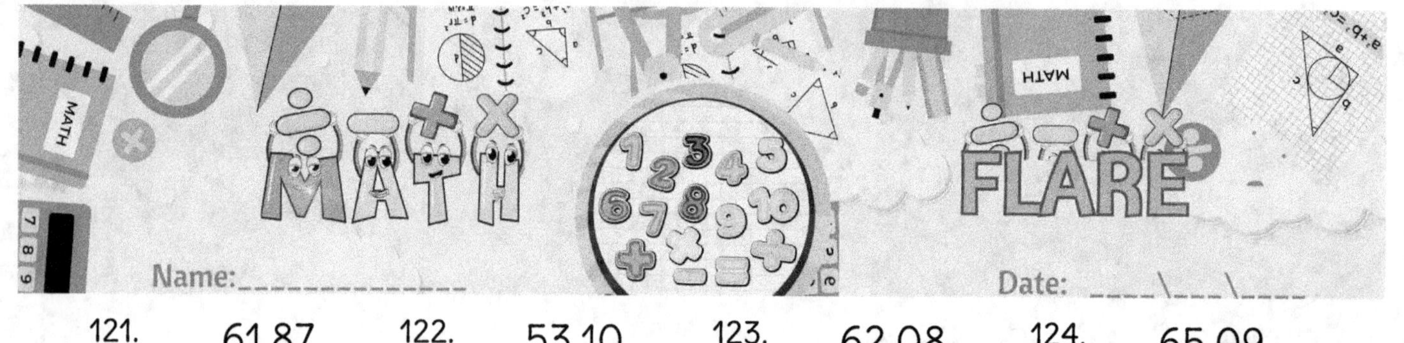

| 121. | 61.87 | 122. | 53.10 | 123. | 62.08 | 124. | 65.09 |
| | − 58.85 | | − 18.38 | | − 19.46 | | − 25.68 |

| 125. | 93.45 | 126. | 52.59 | 127. | 50.71 | 128. | 99.37 |
| | − 80.12 | | − 46.80 | | − 42.47 | | − 63.88 |

| 129. | 50.67 | 130. | 88.95 | 131. | 55.68 | 132. | 31.70 |
| | − 26.03 | | − 60.42 | | − 16.34 | | − 13.12 |

| 133. | 57.86 | 134. | 67.70 | 135. | 76.48 | 136. | 34.08 |
| | − 21.57 | | − 46.06 | | − 43.45 | | − 31.23 |

| 137. | 59.65 | 138. | 99.88 | 139. | 82.14 | 140. | 57.55 |
| | − 47.59 | | − 44.65 | | − 39.04 | | − 51.97 |

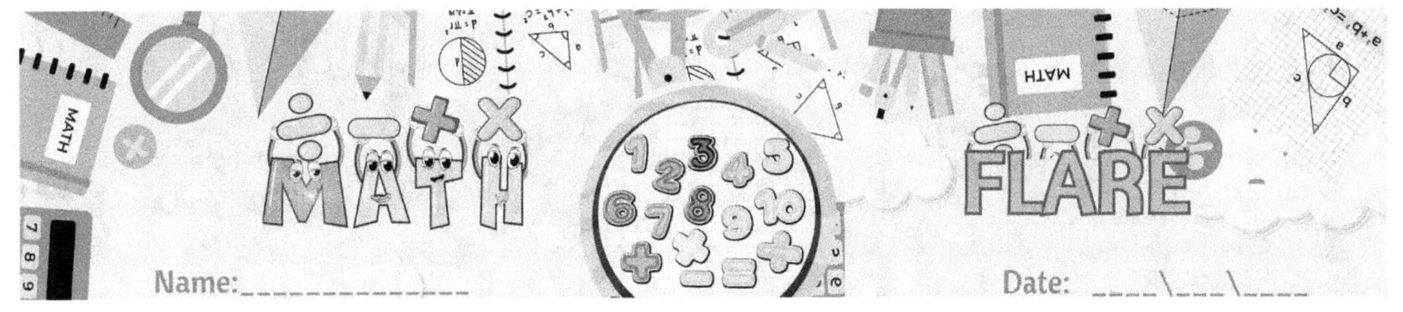

| 141. | 56.00
- 30.48 | 142. | 98.92
- 47.27 | 143. | 90.56
- 42.64 | 144. | 56.86
- 33.50 |

| 145. | 96.68
- 51.64 | 146. | 90.52
- 75.42 | 147. | 62.64
- 13.57 | 148. | 56.10
- 15.46 |

| 149. | 92.02
- 32.26 | 150. | 71.10
- 23.20 | 151. | 39.43
- 30.42 | 152. | 41.65
- 25.74 |

| 153. | 90.05
- 85.94 | 154. | 93.79
- 73.58 | 155. | 52.47
- 43.84 | 156. | 89.38
- 10.58 |

| 157. | 54.12
- 16.71 | 158. | 29.75
- 29.44 | 159. | 67.83
- 30.76 | 160. | 71.53
- 14.78 |

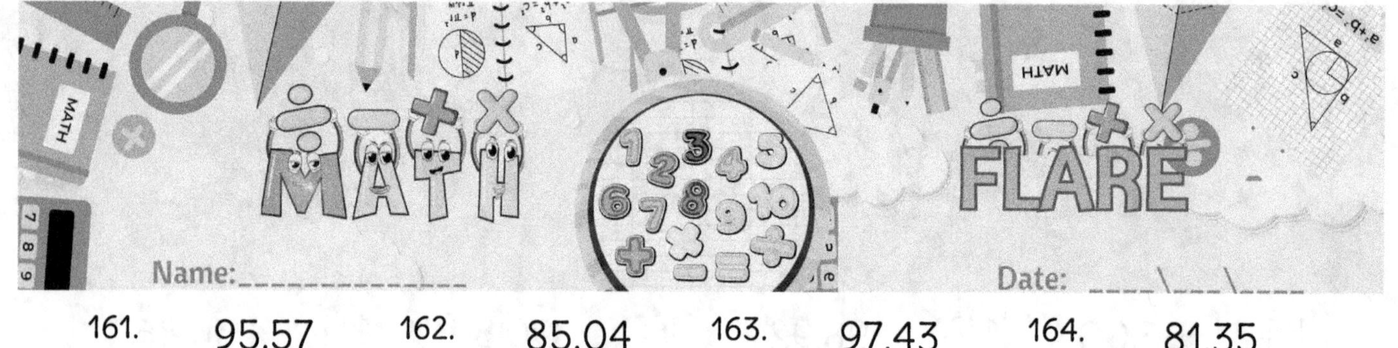

161.   95.57
  − 20.74
	162. 85.04
	  − 23.46
		163. 97.43
		  − 28.01
			164. 81.35
			  − 22.85

165.   69.07
  − 32.71
	166. 95.98
	  − 70.61
		167. 93.95
		  − 10.34
			168. 72.30
			  − 20.69

169.   81.10
  − 62.94
	170. 78.43
	  − 40.16
		171. 73.19
		  − 40.67
			172. 63.45
			  − 41.37

173.   96.01
  − 37.24
	174. 86.93
	  − 58.67
		175. 85.58
		  − 44.46
			176. 92.61
			  − 49.21

177.   67.54
  − 46.64
	178. 26.07
	  − 10.41
		179. 95.73
		  − 61.24
			180. 49.65
			  − 38.40

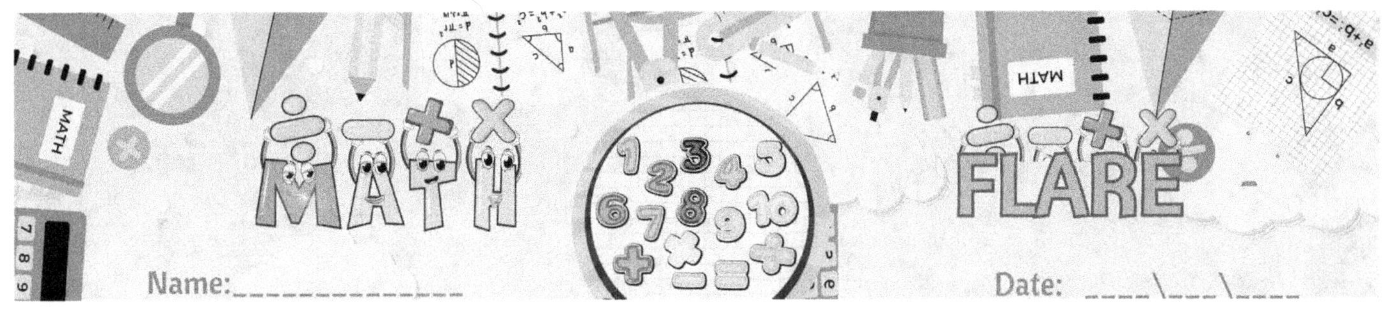

181. 97.62 – 57.17	182. 93.92 – 64.61	183. 62.27 – 37.14	184. 97.22 – 23.63
185. 77.35 – 74.27	186. 47.54 – 33.98	187. 36.13 – 26.80	188. 25.30 – 17.93
189. 95.23 – 55.33	190. 90.81 – 19.12	191. 87.66 – 45.74	192. 19.02 – 17.30
193. 84.34 – 38.40	194. 50.52 – 46.87	195. 72.68 – 65.48	196. 76.96 – 76.44
197. 49.42 – 12.44	198. 83.88 – 72.49	199. 76.82 – 59.68	200. 77.38 – 22.86

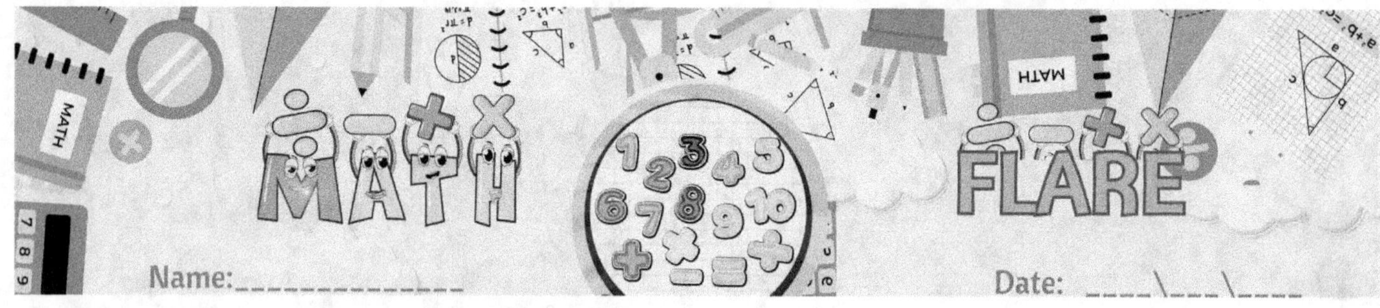

Fraction Identification

Identify fractions of each set of boxes.

201. 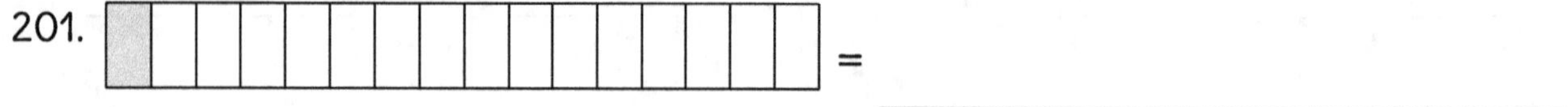 = __________________

202. = __________________

203. = __________________

204. = __________________

205. = __________________

206. = __________________

207. = __________________

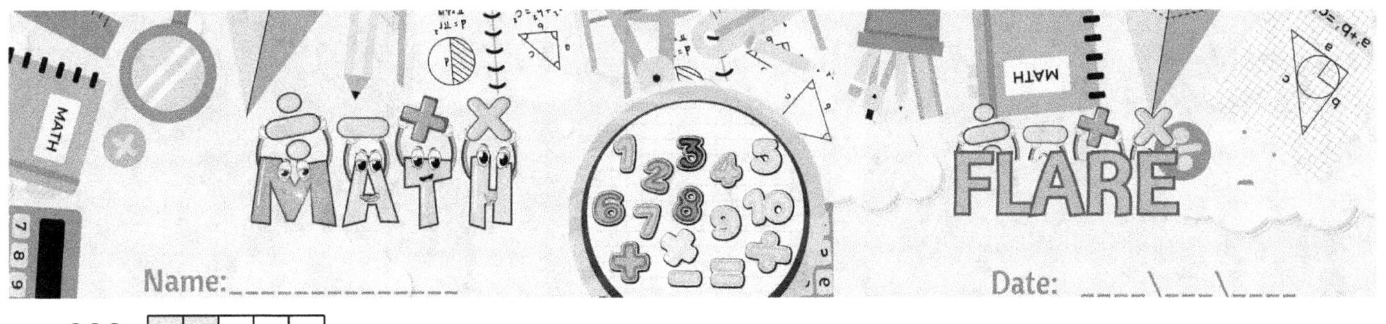

208. 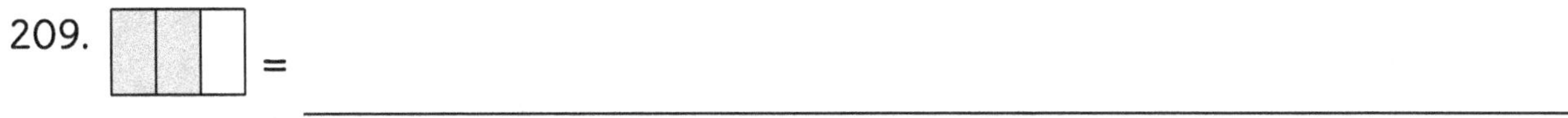 = _______________________________

209. = _______________________________

210.  = _______________________________

211. = _______________________________

212.  = _______________________________

213. = _______________________________

214. 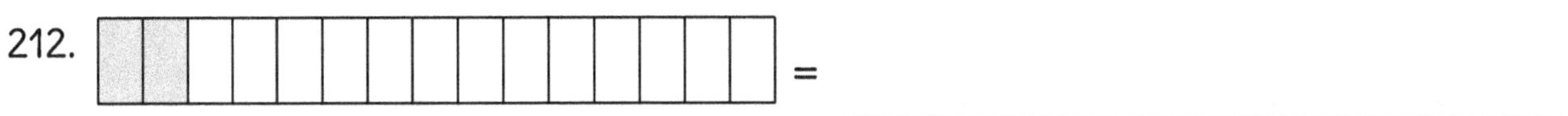 = _______________________________

215. = _______________________________

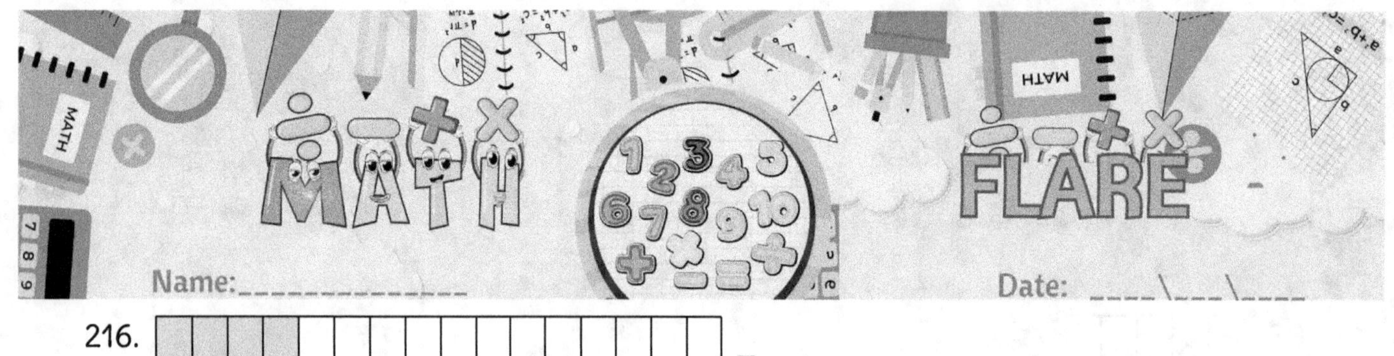

216. 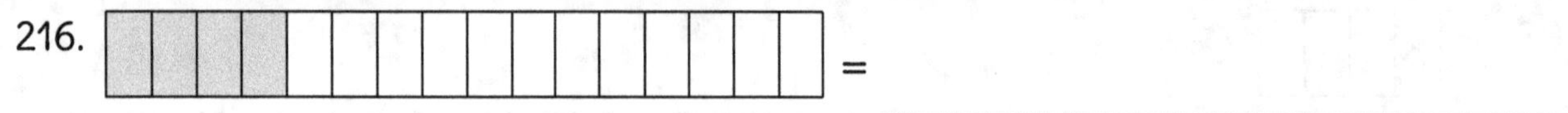 =

____

217. =

____

218. =

____

219.  =

____

220. =

____

221. =

____

222. =

____

223. =

____

224.  = ______________________________

225. = ______________________________

226. = ______________________________

227.  = ______________________________

228. = ______________________________

229. = ______________________________

230. = ______________________________

231.  = ______________________________

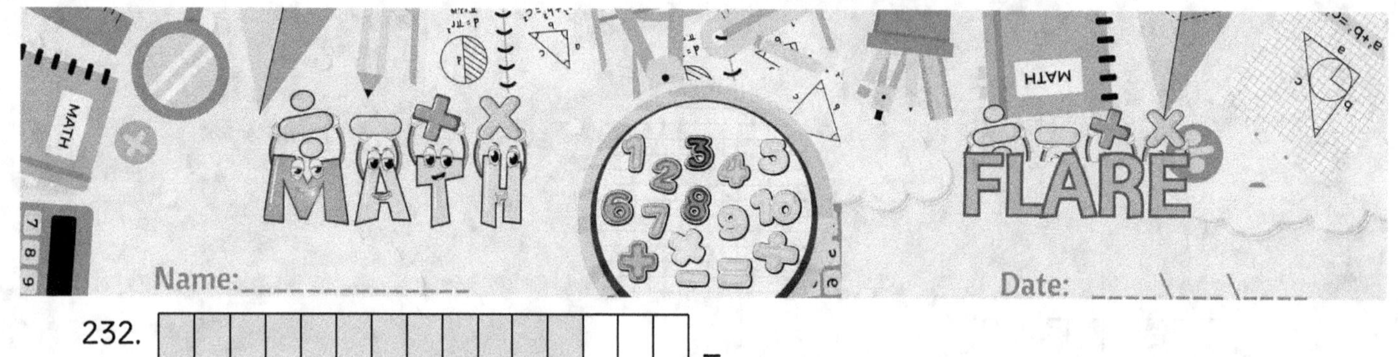

232. 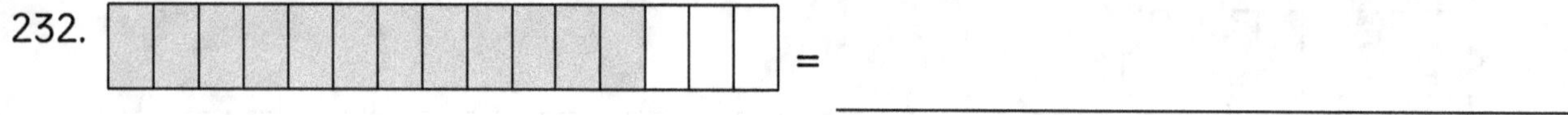 =
____

233. 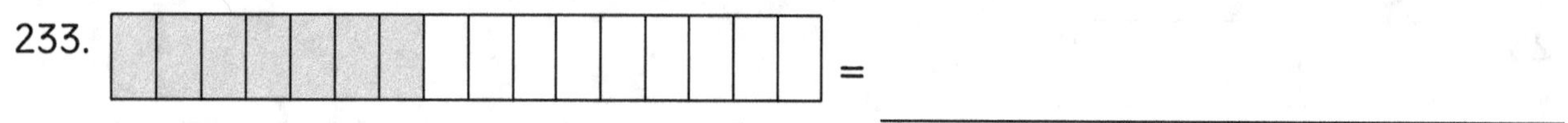 =
____

234. =
____

235. =
____

236. =
____

237. =
____

238. =
____

239. =
____

240. ⬜ =
____

241. ⬜ =
____

242. ⬜ =
____

243. ⬜ =
____

244. ⬜ =
____

245. ⬜ =
____

246. ⬜ =
____

247. ⬜ =
____

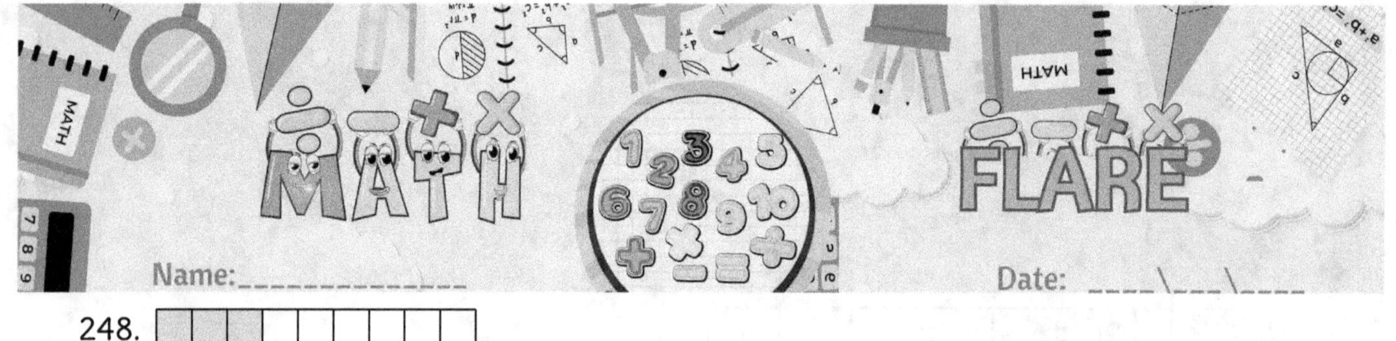

248. = ____________________

249. = ____________________

250. = ____________________

251. = ____________________

252. = ____________________

253. = ____________________

254. = ____________________

255. = ____________________

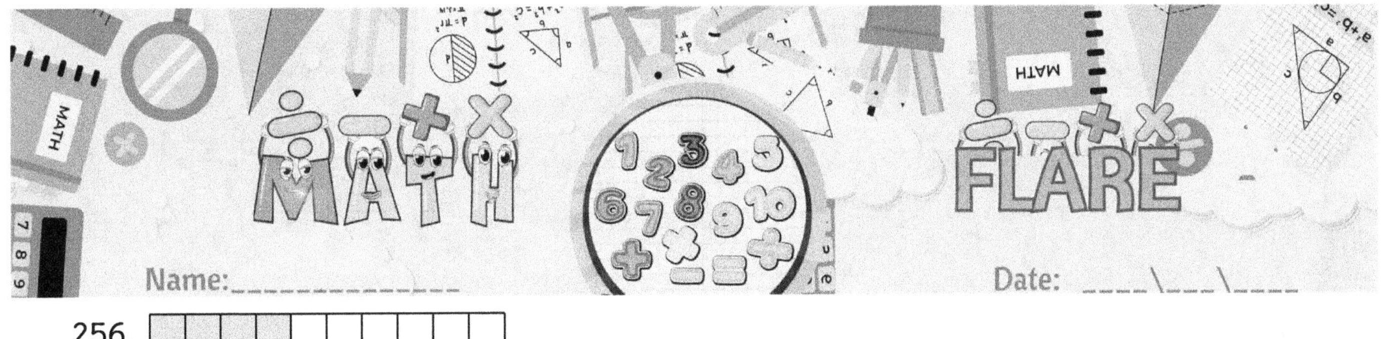

256.  = ___________________________

257. = ___________________________

258. = ___________________________

259. = ___________________________

260. = ___________________________

261. = ___________________________

262. 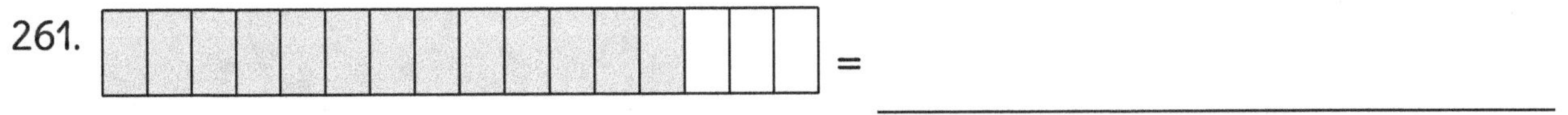 = ___________________________

263. 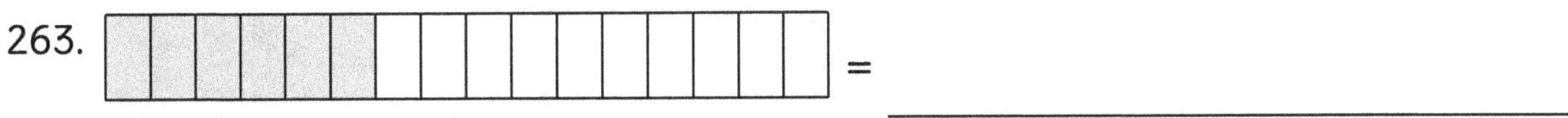 = ___________________________

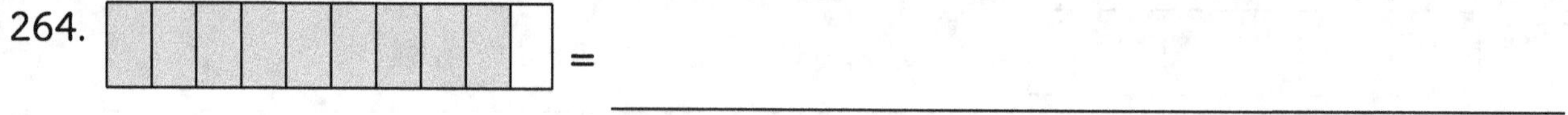

264.   = ______________________________

265.   = ______________________________

266.   = ______________________________

267.   = ______________________________

268.   = ______________________________

269.   = ______________________________

270.   = ______________________________

271.   = ______________________________

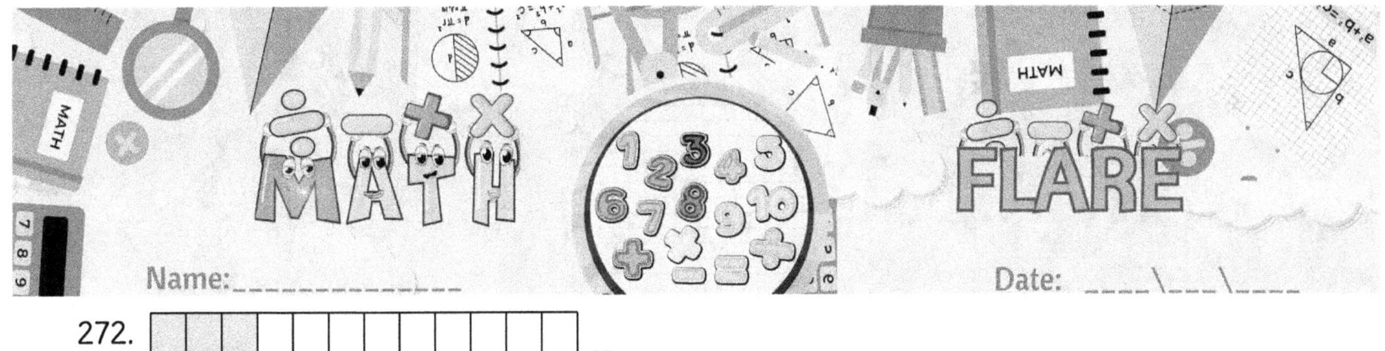

272. =

____

273. =

____

274. =

____

275. =

____

276. =

____

277. =

____

278. =

____

279. =

____

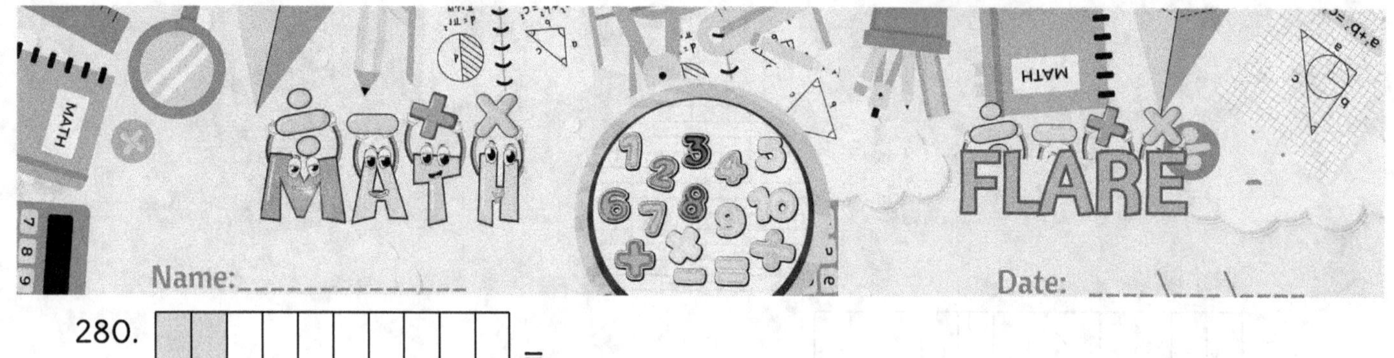

280. = ________________________

281. = ________________________

282. = ________________________

283. = ________________________

284. = ________________________

285. = ________________________

286. = ________________________

287. = ________________________

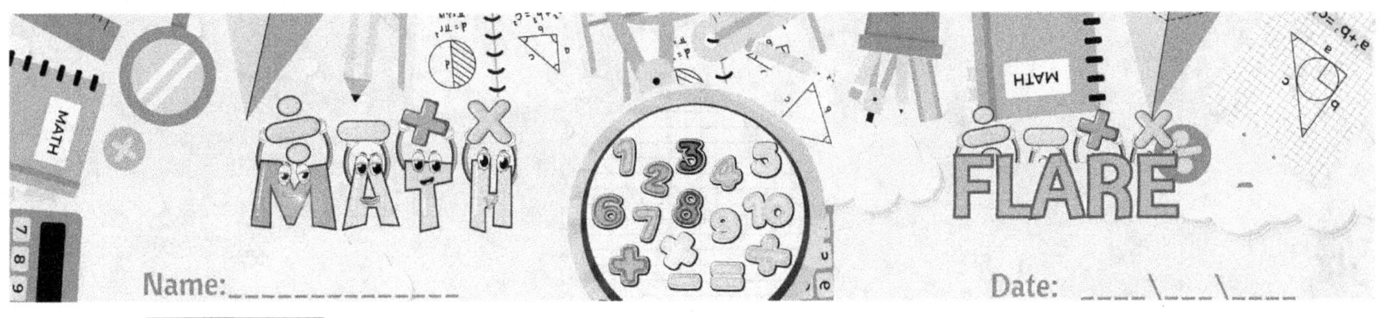

288. ▭ = __________________________

289. ▭ = __________________________

290. ▭ = __________________________

291. ▭ = __________________________

292. ▭ = __________________________

293. ▭ = __________________________

294. ▭ = __________________________

295. ▭ = __________________________

Compare the Fractions

Compare the fractions. Put the signs < , >, or =

296. $\dfrac{1}{17}$ ___ $\dfrac{4}{17}$

297. $\dfrac{5}{21}$ ___ $\dfrac{3}{21}$

298. $\dfrac{28}{40}$ ___ $\dfrac{105}{40}$

299. $\dfrac{70}{75}$ ___ $\dfrac{142}{75}$

300. $\dfrac{6}{8}$ ___ $\dfrac{5}{8}$

301. $\dfrac{8}{16}$ ___ $\dfrac{2}{16}$

302. $\dfrac{4}{5}$ ___ $\dfrac{3}{5}$

303. $\dfrac{5}{30}$ ___ $\dfrac{59}{30}$

304. $\dfrac{18}{39}$ ___ $\dfrac{5}{39}$

305. $\dfrac{22}{14}$ ___ $\dfrac{5}{14}$

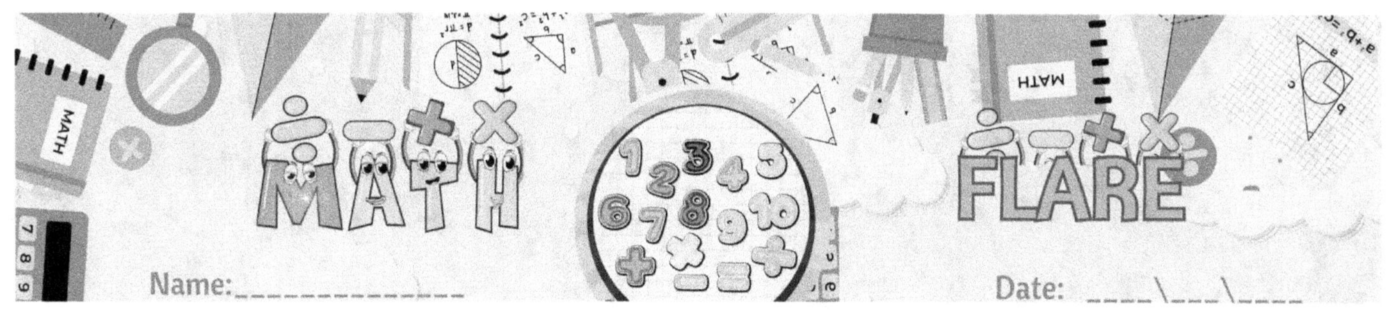

306. $\dfrac{14}{22}$ ___ $\dfrac{3}{22}$

307. $\dfrac{120}{138}$ ___ $\dfrac{313}{138}$

308. $\dfrac{28}{32}$ ___ $\dfrac{10}{32}$

309. $\dfrac{32}{11}$ ___ $\dfrac{1}{11}$

310. $\dfrac{5}{12}$ ___ $\dfrac{31}{12}$

311. $\dfrac{3}{2}$ ___ $\dfrac{1}{2}$

312. $\dfrac{5}{3}$ ___ $\dfrac{4}{3}$

313. $\dfrac{6}{18}$ ___ $\dfrac{49}{18}$

314. $\dfrac{19}{7}$ ___ $\dfrac{5}{7}$

315. $\dfrac{69}{25}$ ___ $\dfrac{26}{25}$

316. $\dfrac{18}{57}$ ___ $\dfrac{12}{57}$

317. $\dfrac{45}{16}$ ___ $\dfrac{33}{16}$

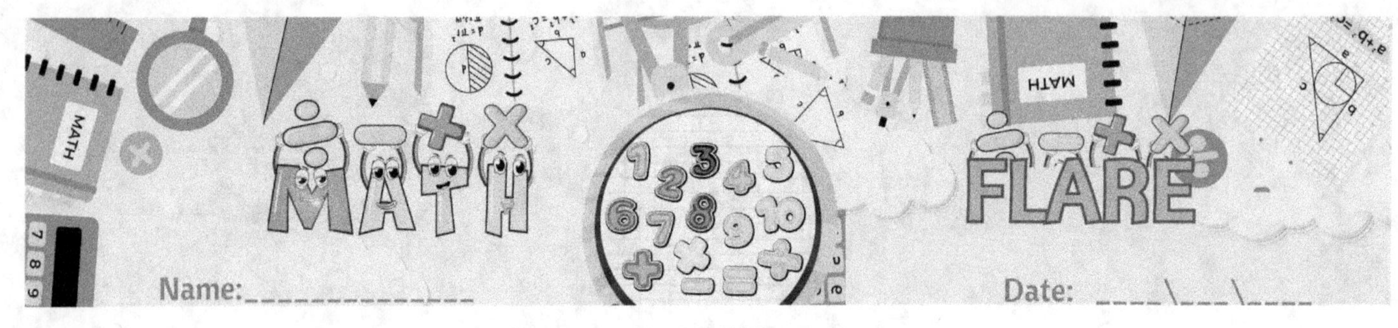

318. $\dfrac{8}{40}$ ___ $\dfrac{39}{40}$

319. $\dfrac{1}{4}$ ___ $\dfrac{1}{4}$

320. $\dfrac{12}{13}$ ___ $\dfrac{9}{13}$

321. $\dfrac{15}{9}$ ___ $\dfrac{3}{9}$

322. $\dfrac{50}{60}$ ___ $\dfrac{167}{60}$

323. $\dfrac{28}{38}$ ___ $\dfrac{18}{38}$

324. $\dfrac{5}{6}$ ___ $\dfrac{7}{6}$

325. $\dfrac{6}{14}$ ___ $\dfrac{3}{14}$

326. $\dfrac{20}{25}$ ___ $\dfrac{8}{25}$

327. $\dfrac{49}{17}$ ___ $\dfrac{30}{17}$

328. $\dfrac{26}{18}$ ___ $\dfrac{14}{18}$

329. $\dfrac{20}{40}$ ___ $\dfrac{61}{40}$

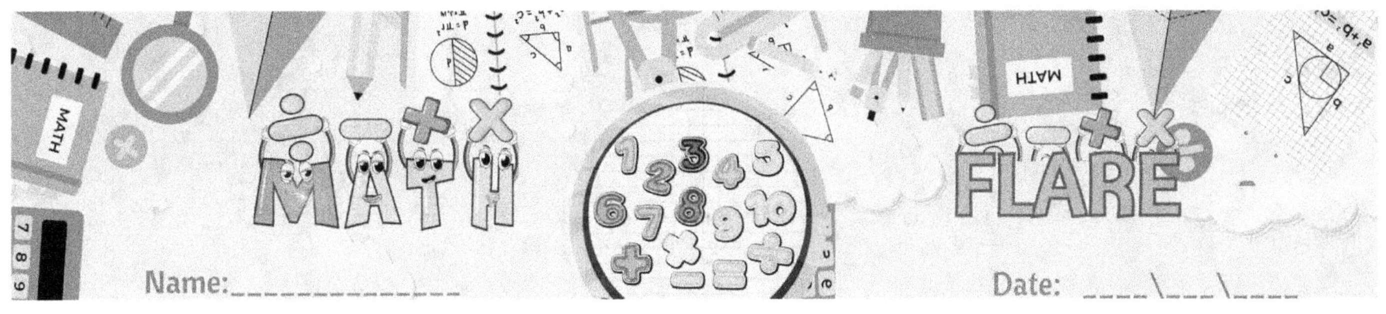

Name:_______________   Date: _______________

330. $\dfrac{49}{21}$ ___ $\dfrac{3}{21}$

331. $\dfrac{19}{24}$ ___ $\dfrac{44}{24}$

332. $\dfrac{4}{12}$ ___ $\dfrac{10}{12}$

333. $\dfrac{10}{8}$ ___ $\dfrac{2}{8}$

334. $\dfrac{46}{30}$ ___ $\dfrac{22}{30}$

335. $\dfrac{5}{25}$ ___ $\dfrac{18}{25}$

336. $\dfrac{19}{15}$ ___ $\dfrac{29}{15}$

337. $\dfrac{3}{6}$ ___ $\dfrac{1}{6}$

338. $\dfrac{84}{92}$ ___ $\dfrac{87}{92}$

339. $\dfrac{17}{14}$ ___ $\dfrac{4}{14}$

340. $\dfrac{15}{66}$ ___ $\dfrac{160}{66}$

341. $\dfrac{10}{20}$ ___ $\dfrac{14}{20}$

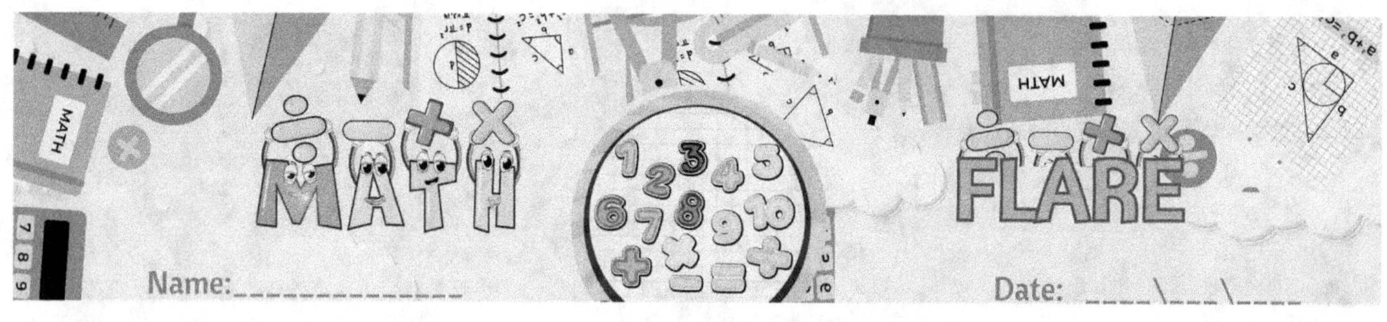

342. $\dfrac{8}{21}$ ___ $\dfrac{31}{21}$

343. $\dfrac{12}{16}$ ___ $\dfrac{11}{16}$

344. $\dfrac{46}{24}$ ___ $\dfrac{16}{24}$

345. $\dfrac{1}{3}$ ___ $\dfrac{1}{3}$

346. $\dfrac{29}{30}$ ___ $\dfrac{51}{30}$

347. $\dfrac{26}{12}$ ___ $\dfrac{4}{12}$

348. $\dfrac{24}{54}$ ___ $\dfrac{7}{54}$

349. $\dfrac{6}{12}$ ___ $\dfrac{31}{12}$

350. $\dfrac{7}{13}$ ___ $\dfrac{17}{13}$

351. $\dfrac{3}{4}$ ___ $\dfrac{3}{4}$

352. $\dfrac{6}{132}$ ___ $\dfrac{15}{132}$

353. $\dfrac{13}{9}$ ___ $\dfrac{3}{9}$

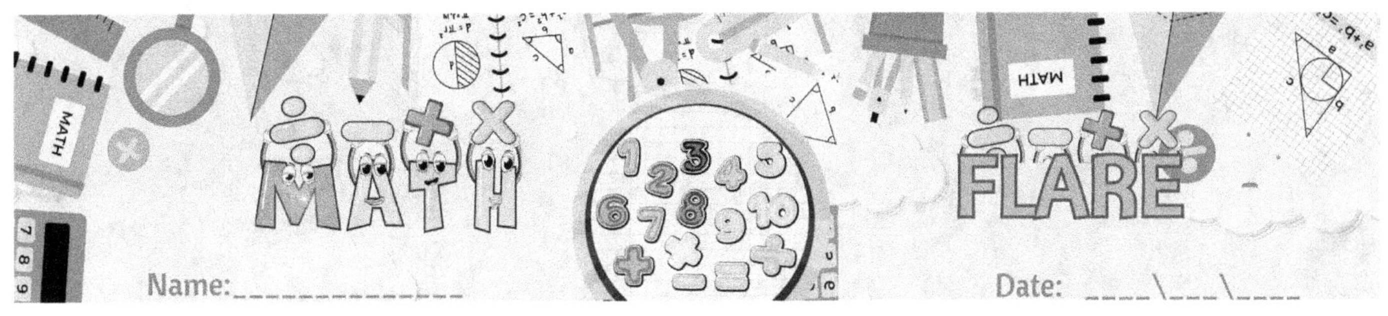

354. $\dfrac{2}{5}$ ___ $\dfrac{11}{5}$

355. $\dfrac{14}{10}$ ___ $\dfrac{3}{10}$

356. $\dfrac{17}{23}$ ___ $\dfrac{13}{23}$

357. $\dfrac{50}{70}$ ___ $\dfrac{37}{70}$

358. $\dfrac{10}{38}$ ___ $\dfrac{37}{38}$

359. $\dfrac{8}{15}$ ___ $\dfrac{43}{15}$

360. $\dfrac{2}{17}$ ___ $\dfrac{28}{17}$

361. $\dfrac{31}{11}$ ___ $\dfrac{28}{11}$

362. $\dfrac{4}{8}$ ___ $\dfrac{3}{8}$

363. $\dfrac{2}{12}$ ___ $\dfrac{8}{12}$

364. $\dfrac{24}{50}$ ___ $\dfrac{77}{50}$

365. $\dfrac{30}{42}$ ___ $\dfrac{21}{42}$

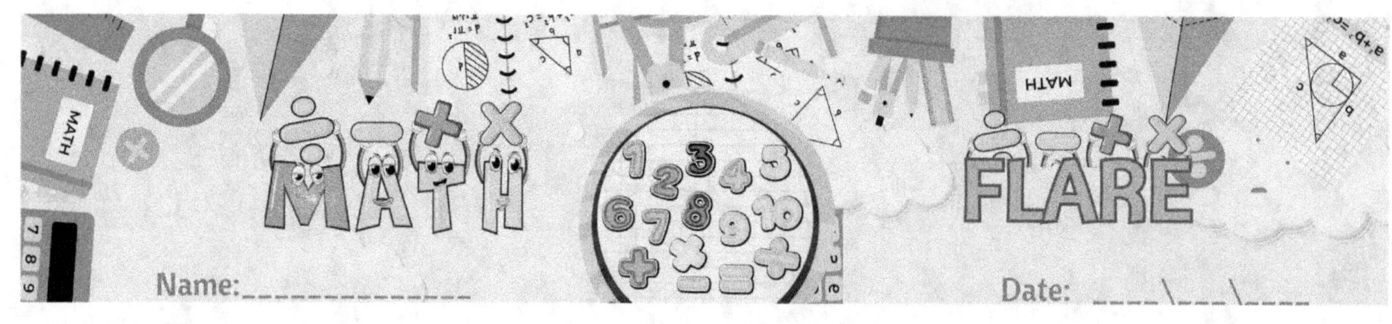

366. $\dfrac{18}{48}$ ___ $\dfrac{2}{48}$

367. $\dfrac{21}{24}$ ___ $\dfrac{7}{24}$

368. $\dfrac{4}{5}$ ___ $\dfrac{2}{5}$

369. $\dfrac{1}{19}$ ___ $\dfrac{21}{19}$

370. $\dfrac{7}{9}$ ___ $\dfrac{12}{9}$

371. $\dfrac{18}{17}$ ___ $\dfrac{14}{17}$

372. $\dfrac{42}{22}$ ___ $\dfrac{56}{22}$

373. $\dfrac{18}{126}$ ___ $\dfrac{112}{126}$

374. $\dfrac{15}{125}$ ___ $\dfrac{237}{125}$

375. $\dfrac{28}{11}$ ___ $\dfrac{20}{11}$

376. $\dfrac{2}{4}$ ___ $\dfrac{10}{4}$

377. $\dfrac{48}{23}$ ___ $\dfrac{68}{23}$

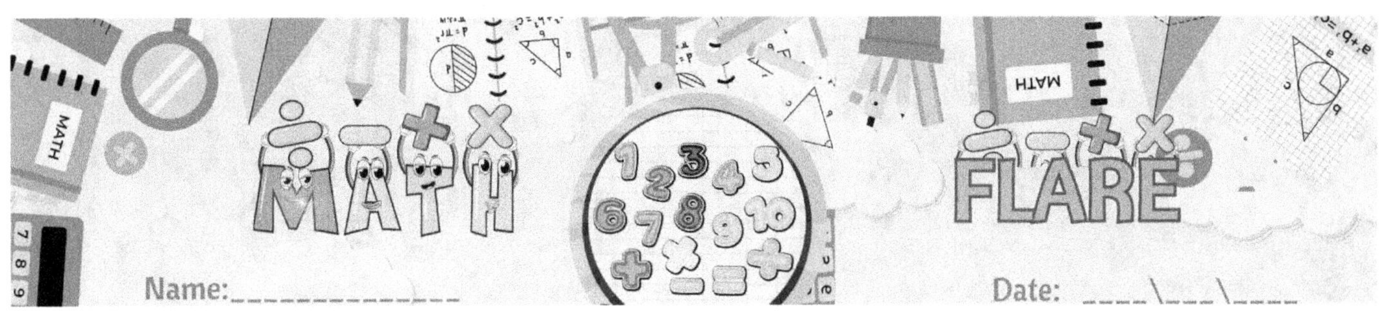

378. $\dfrac{15}{18}$ ___ $\dfrac{13}{18}$

379. $\dfrac{24}{60}$ ___ $\dfrac{18}{60}$

380. $\dfrac{11}{14}$ ___ $\dfrac{22}{14}$

381. $\dfrac{10}{75}$ ___ $\dfrac{41}{75}$

382. $\dfrac{22}{16}$ ___ $\dfrac{28}{16}$

383. $\dfrac{2}{14}$ ___ $\dfrac{10}{14}$

384. $\dfrac{14}{18}$ ___ $\dfrac{43}{18}$

385. $\dfrac{42}{60}$ ___ $\dfrac{135}{60}$

386. $\dfrac{6}{10}$ ___ $\dfrac{3}{10}$

387. $\dfrac{6}{4}$ ___ $\dfrac{7}{4}$

388. $\dfrac{66}{72}$ ___ $\dfrac{50}{72}$

389. $\dfrac{35}{65}$ ___ $\dfrac{54}{65}$

390. $\dfrac{19}{24} \underline{} \dfrac{56}{24}$

391. $\dfrac{12}{24} \underline{} \dfrac{31}{24}$

392. $\dfrac{35}{18} \underline{} \dfrac{41}{18}$

393. $\dfrac{66}{72} \underline{} \dfrac{14}{72}$

394. $\dfrac{1}{5} \underline{} \dfrac{11}{5}$

395. $\dfrac{1}{2} \underline{} \dfrac{1}{2}$

396. $\dfrac{40}{16} \underline{} \dfrac{40}{16}$

397. $\dfrac{24}{20} \underline{} \dfrac{13}{20}$

398. $\dfrac{5}{9} \underline{} \dfrac{5}{9}$

399. $\dfrac{9}{18} \underline{} \dfrac{15}{18}$

400. $\dfrac{56}{84} \underline{} \dfrac{78}{84}$

401. $\dfrac{21}{11} \underline{} \dfrac{9}{11}$

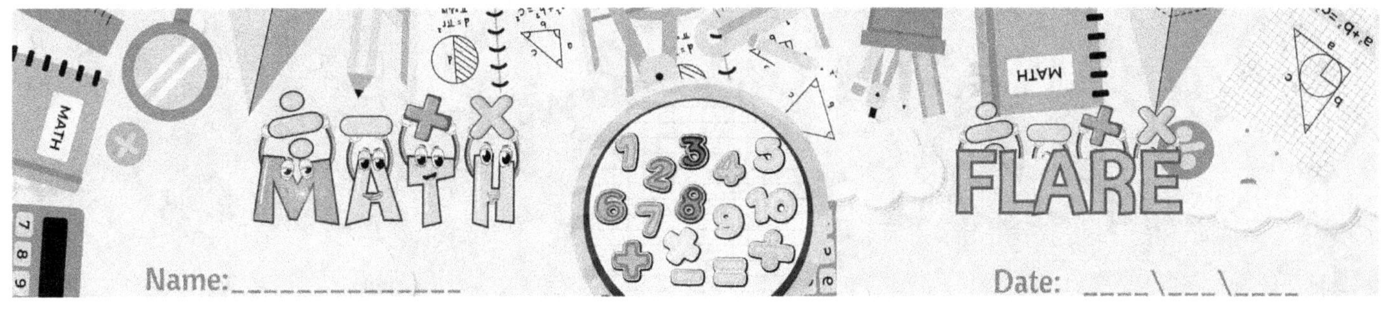

Equivalent Fractions

402. $\dfrac{14}{16} = \dfrac{98}{}$

403. $\dfrac{8}{} = \dfrac{40}{45}$

404. $\dfrac{1}{6} = \dfrac{}{12}$

405. $\dfrac{1}{2} = \dfrac{6}{}$

406. $\dfrac{}{13} = \dfrac{45}{117}$

407. $\dfrac{2}{4} = \dfrac{6}{}$

408. $\dfrac{2}{3} = \dfrac{6}{}$

409. $\dfrac{1}{11} = \dfrac{}{110}$

410. $\dfrac{2}{8} = \dfrac{6}{}$

411. $\dfrac{17}{} = \dfrac{119}{126}$

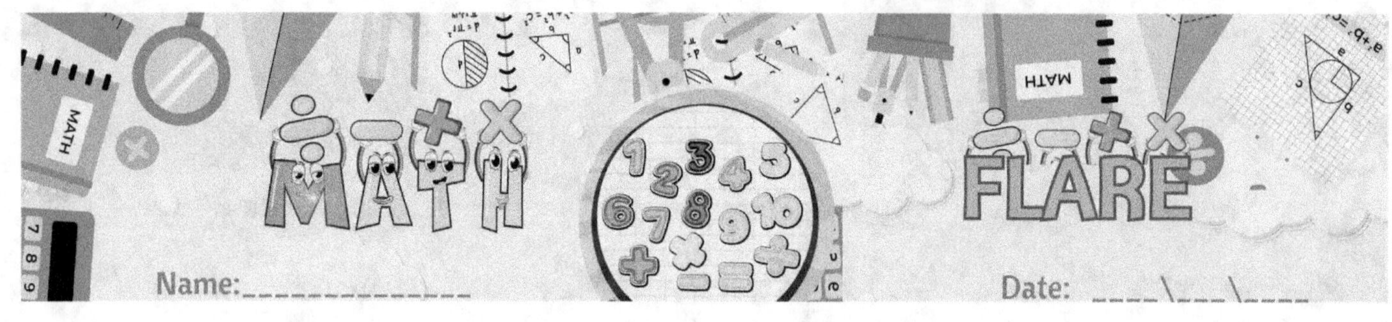

412. $\dfrac{7}{19} = \dfrac{}{95}$

413. $\dfrac{5}{} = \dfrac{15}{30}$

414. $\dfrac{1}{} = \dfrac{8}{32}$

415. $\dfrac{}{12} = \dfrac{70}{120}$

416. $\dfrac{14}{15} = \dfrac{112}{}$

417. $\dfrac{7}{} = \dfrac{21}{30}$

418. $\dfrac{9}{13} = \dfrac{36}{}$

419. $\dfrac{6}{} = \dfrac{36}{42}$

420. $\dfrac{8}{18} = \dfrac{56}{}$

421. $\dfrac{14}{19} = \dfrac{}{190}$

422. $\dfrac{3}{} = \dfrac{24}{48}$

423. $\dfrac{}{2} = \dfrac{7}{14}$

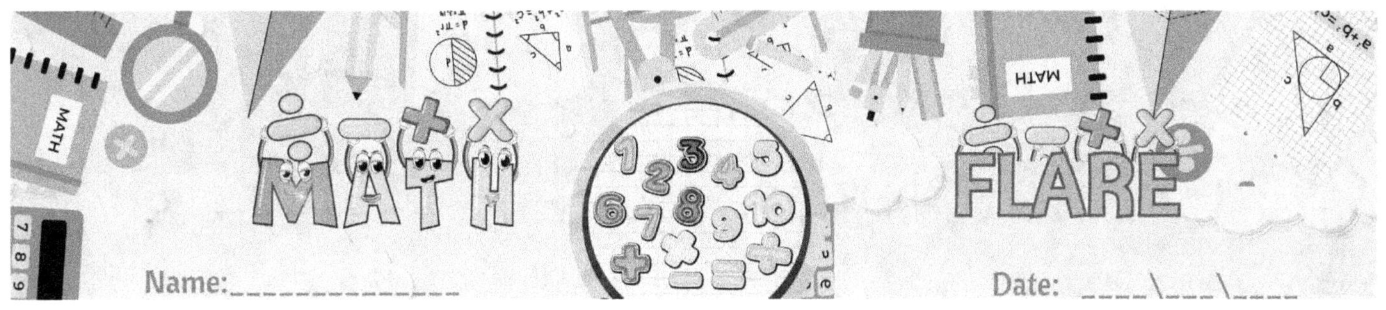

Name:__________________   Date: _______________

424. $\dfrac{4}{8} = \dfrac{}{64}$

425. $\dfrac{1}{} = \dfrac{8}{24}$

426. $\dfrac{12}{} = \dfrac{96}{112}$

427. $\dfrac{2}{} = \dfrac{4}{10}$

428. $\dfrac{2}{} = \dfrac{14}{77}$

429. $\dfrac{}{16} = \dfrac{48}{96}$

430. $\dfrac{13}{} = \dfrac{91}{140}$

431. $\dfrac{}{9} = \dfrac{12}{36}$

432. $\dfrac{15}{17} = \dfrac{135}{}$

433. $\dfrac{1}{2} = \dfrac{2}{}$

434. $\dfrac{1}{3} = \dfrac{6}{}$

435. $\dfrac{}{11} = \dfrac{16}{22}$

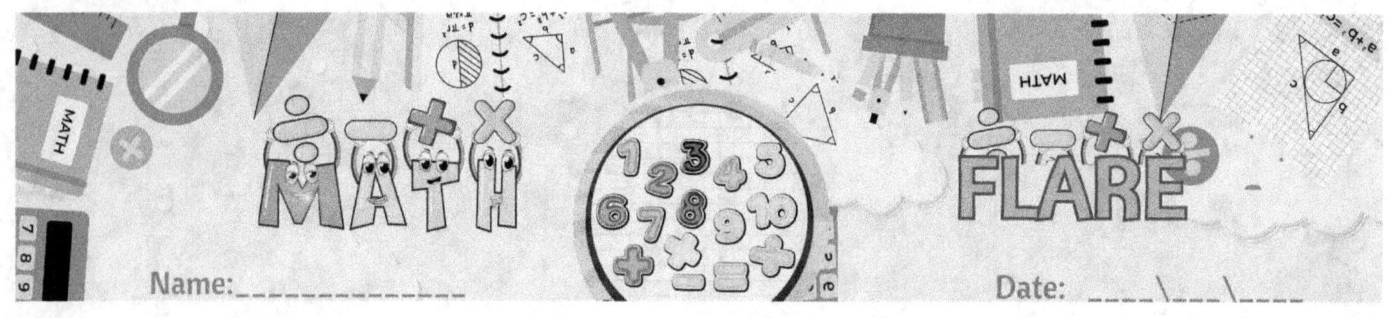

436. $\dfrac{}{20} = \dfrac{24}{160}$

437. $\dfrac{}{7} = \dfrac{24}{28}$

438. $\dfrac{2}{} = \dfrac{12}{96}$

439. $\dfrac{7}{8} = \dfrac{}{64}$

440. $\dfrac{}{10} = \dfrac{18}{90}$

441. $\dfrac{2}{16} = \dfrac{}{32}$

442. $\dfrac{2}{} = \dfrac{10}{85}$

443. $\dfrac{18}{19} = \dfrac{144}{}$

444. $\dfrac{}{2} = \dfrac{8}{16}$

445. $\dfrac{5}{6} = \dfrac{30}{}$

446. $\dfrac{1}{10} = \dfrac{}{90}$

447. $\dfrac{}{14} = \dfrac{12}{84}$

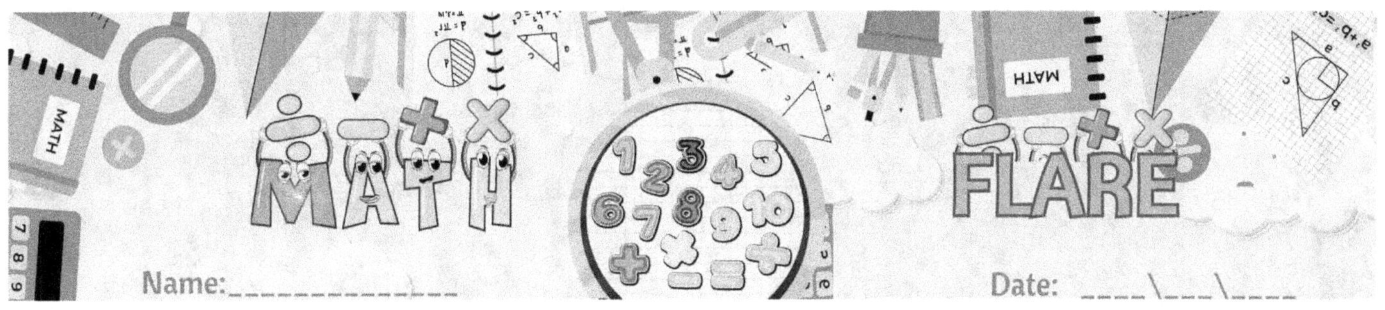

448. $\dfrac{1}{} = \dfrac{4}{60}$

449. $\dfrac{13}{} = \dfrac{117}{180}$

450. $\dfrac{16}{18} = \dfrac{}{162}$

451. $\dfrac{}{11} = \dfrac{3}{33}$

452. $\dfrac{}{4} = \dfrac{14}{28}$

453. $\dfrac{}{7} = \dfrac{16}{28}$

454. $\dfrac{}{8} = \dfrac{9}{24}$

455. $\dfrac{1}{3} = \dfrac{}{6}$

456. $\dfrac{2}{} = \dfrac{14}{35}$

457. $\dfrac{}{12} = \dfrac{45}{60}$

458. $\dfrac{4}{9} = \dfrac{}{81}$

459. $\dfrac{1}{5} = \dfrac{}{45}$

Fractions Addition: Common Denominator

Find the sum.

460. $\frac{6}{12} + \frac{5}{12} =$ _______________

461. $\frac{5}{12} + \frac{3}{12} =$ _______________

462. $\frac{1}{3} + \frac{1}{3} =$ _______________

463. $\frac{1}{9} + \frac{6}{9} =$ _______________

464. $\frac{1}{6} + \frac{4}{6} =$ _______________

465. $\frac{6}{8} + \frac{1}{8} =$ _______________

466. $\frac{1}{2} + \frac{1}{2} =$ _______________

467. $\frac{1}{5} + \frac{1}{5} =$ _______________

468. $\frac{5}{10} + \frac{3}{10} =$ _______________

469. $\frac{2}{4} + \frac{1}{4} =$ _______________

470. $\frac{3}{7} + \frac{1}{7} =$ _______________

471. $\frac{1}{11} + \frac{9}{11} =$ _______________

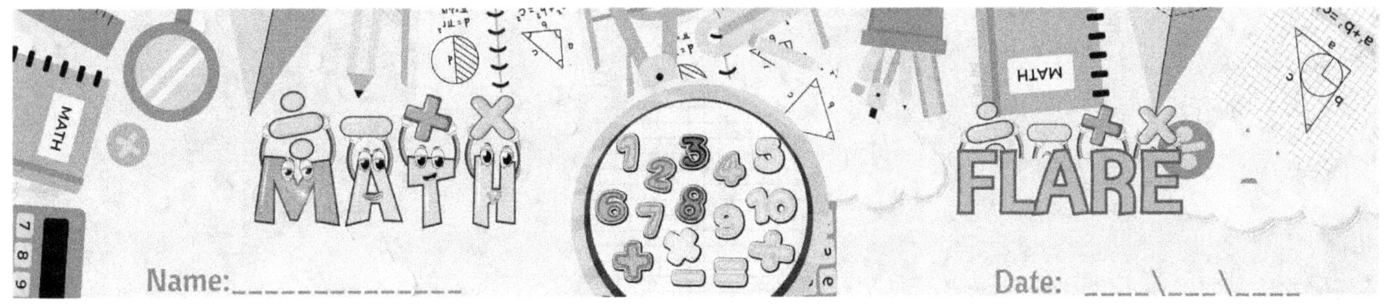

Name:_______________   Date: ____________

472. $\frac{3}{6} + \frac{1}{6}$ = _________________

473. $\frac{4}{11} + \frac{2}{11}$ = _________________

474. $\frac{3}{9} + \frac{4}{9}$ = _________________

475. $\frac{5}{10} + \frac{2}{10}$ = _________________

476. $\frac{3}{8} + \frac{2}{8}$ = _________________

477. $\frac{2}{5} + \frac{2}{5}$ = _________________

478. $\frac{1}{6} + \frac{2}{6}$ = _________________

479. $\frac{1}{4} + \frac{2}{4}$ = _________________

480. $\frac{5}{7} + \frac{1}{7}$ = _________________

481. $\frac{2}{6} + \frac{3}{6}$ = _________________

482. $\frac{1}{9} + \frac{4}{9}$ = _________________

483. $\frac{6}{10} + \frac{1}{10}$ = _________________

484. $\frac{4}{8} + \frac{3}{8}$ = _________________

485. $\frac{3}{12} + \frac{3}{12}$ = _________________

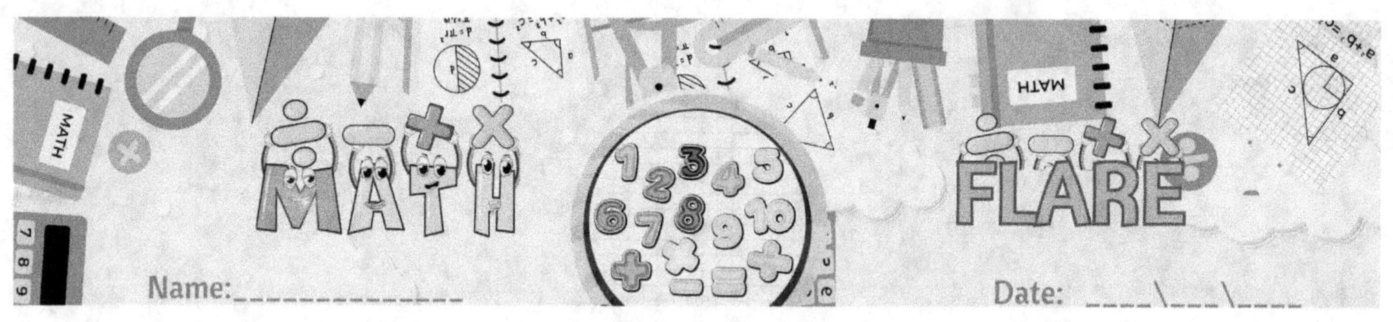

486. $\dfrac{1}{11} + \dfrac{7}{11} =$ _______________

487. $\dfrac{3}{7} + \dfrac{3}{7} =$ _______________

488. $\dfrac{1}{8} + \dfrac{1}{8} =$ _______________

489. $\dfrac{3}{10} + \dfrac{4}{10} =$ _______________

490. $\dfrac{1}{4} + \dfrac{1}{4} =$ _______________

491. $\dfrac{5}{9} + \dfrac{3}{9} =$ _______________

492. $\dfrac{4}{12} + \dfrac{2}{12} =$ _______________

493. $\dfrac{1}{7} + \dfrac{3}{7} =$ _______________

494. $\dfrac{8}{11} + \dfrac{2}{11} =$ _______________

495. $\dfrac{1}{7} + \dfrac{1}{7} =$ _______________

496. $\dfrac{3}{6} + \dfrac{2}{6} =$ _______________

497. $\dfrac{9}{11} + \dfrac{1}{11} =$ _______________

498. $\dfrac{1}{12} + \dfrac{2}{12} =$ _______________

499. $\dfrac{5}{9} + \dfrac{2}{9} =$ _______________

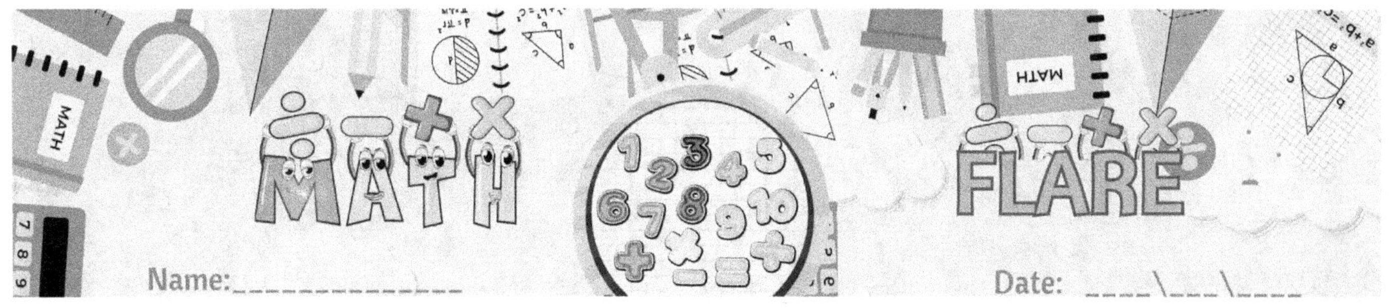

500. $\frac{1}{8} + \frac{2}{8} =$ _______________

501. $\frac{2}{10} + \frac{2}{10} =$ _______________

502. $\frac{3}{11} + \frac{6}{11} =$ _______________

503. $\frac{2}{8} + \frac{4}{8} =$ _______________

504. $\frac{3}{10} + \frac{1}{10} =$ _______________

505. $\frac{10}{12} + \frac{1}{12} =$ _______________

506. $\frac{2}{5} + \frac{1}{5} =$ _______________

507. $\frac{4}{9} + \frac{4}{9} =$ _______________

508. $\frac{6}{12} + \frac{4}{12} =$ _______________

509. $\frac{4}{6} + \frac{1}{6} =$ _______________

510. $\frac{1}{10} + \frac{8}{10} =$ _______________

511. $\frac{2}{7} + \frac{3}{7} =$ _______________

512. $\frac{4}{9} + \frac{3}{9} =$ _______________

513. $\frac{1}{11} + \frac{3}{11} =$ _______________

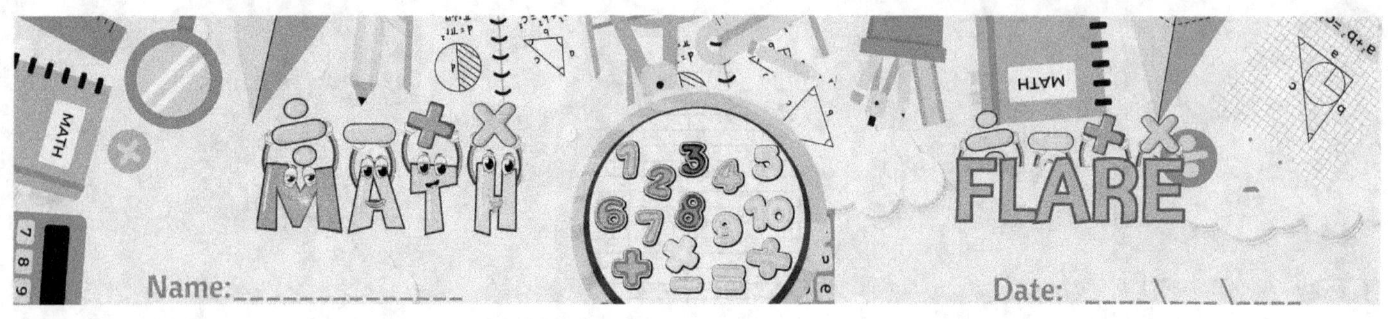

514. $\dfrac{2}{10} + \dfrac{7}{10} =$ _______________

515. $\dfrac{1}{9} + \dfrac{3}{9} =$ _______________

516. $\dfrac{3}{5} + \dfrac{1}{5} =$ _______________

517. $\dfrac{1}{11} + \dfrac{2}{11} =$ _______________

518. $\dfrac{2}{12} + \dfrac{3}{12} =$ _______________

519. $\dfrac{3}{7} + \dfrac{2}{7} =$ _______________

520. $\dfrac{6}{9} + \dfrac{1}{9} =$ _______________

521. $\dfrac{7}{12} + \dfrac{1}{12} =$ _______________

522. $\dfrac{1}{5} + \dfrac{3}{5} =$ _______________

523. $\dfrac{2}{8} + \dfrac{5}{8} =$ _______________

524. $\dfrac{1}{10} + \dfrac{6}{10} =$ _______________

525. $\dfrac{2}{11} + \dfrac{2}{11} =$ _______________

526. $\dfrac{1}{7} + \dfrac{5}{7} =$ _______________

527. $\dfrac{2}{12} + \dfrac{6}{12} =$ _______________

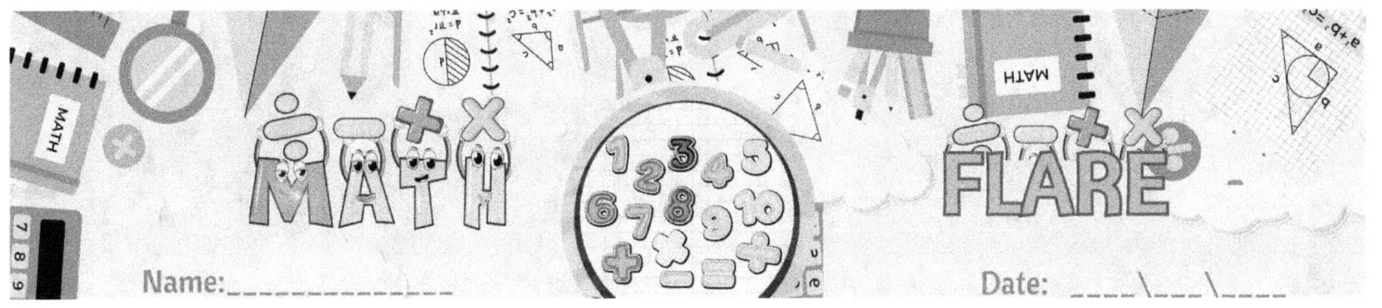

528. $\frac{3}{9} + \frac{1}{9} =$ ______

529. $\frac{4}{8} + \frac{2}{8} =$ ______

530. $\frac{1}{6} + \frac{3}{6} =$ ______

531. $\frac{4}{11} + \frac{1}{11} =$ ______

532. $\frac{3}{8} + \frac{1}{8} =$ ______

533. $\frac{4}{12} + \frac{6}{12} =$ ______

534. $\frac{2}{10} + \frac{6}{10} =$ ______

535. $\frac{1}{5} + \frac{2}{5} =$ ______

536. $\frac{2}{12} + \frac{7}{12} =$ ______

537. $\frac{6}{11} + \frac{2}{11} =$ ______

538. $\frac{3}{8} + \frac{4}{8} =$ ______

539. $\frac{9}{12} + \frac{2}{12} =$ ______

540. $\frac{7}{11} + \frac{1}{11} =$ ______

541. $\frac{3}{10} + \frac{6}{10} =$ ______

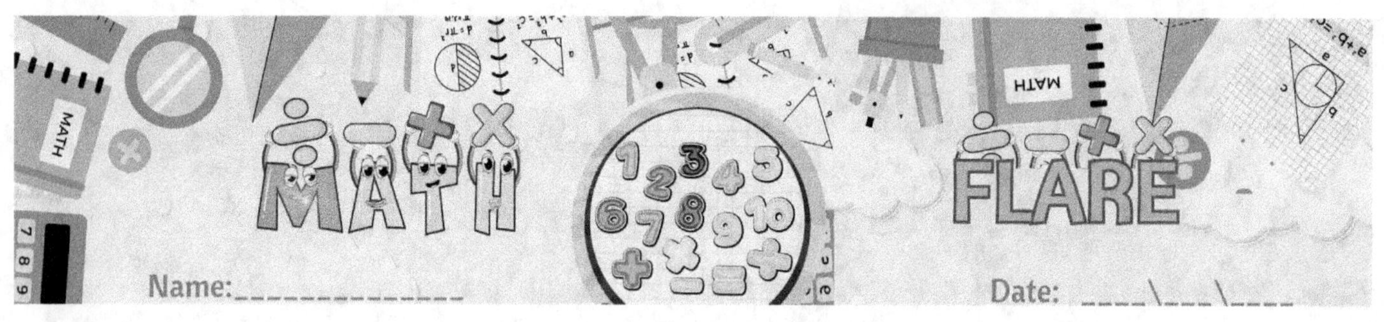

542. $\dfrac{2}{9} + \dfrac{1}{9} =$ _______________

543. $\dfrac{2}{9} + \dfrac{5}{9} =$ _______________

544. $\dfrac{1}{8} + \dfrac{6}{8} =$ _______________

545. $\dfrac{3}{11} + \dfrac{4}{11} =$ _______________

546. $\dfrac{2}{7} + \dfrac{4}{7} =$ _______________

547. $\dfrac{3}{12} + \dfrac{6}{12} =$ _______________

548. $\dfrac{2}{10} + \dfrac{4}{10} =$ _______________

549. $\dfrac{3}{12} + \dfrac{2}{12} =$ _______________

550. $\dfrac{3}{8} + \dfrac{3}{8} =$ _______________

551. $\dfrac{1}{10} + \dfrac{4}{10} =$ _______________

552. $\dfrac{2}{9} + \dfrac{3}{9} =$ _______________

553. $\dfrac{3}{12} + \dfrac{7}{12} =$ _______________

554. $\dfrac{2}{11} + \dfrac{6}{11} =$ _______________

555. $\dfrac{2}{6} + \dfrac{2}{6} =$ _______________

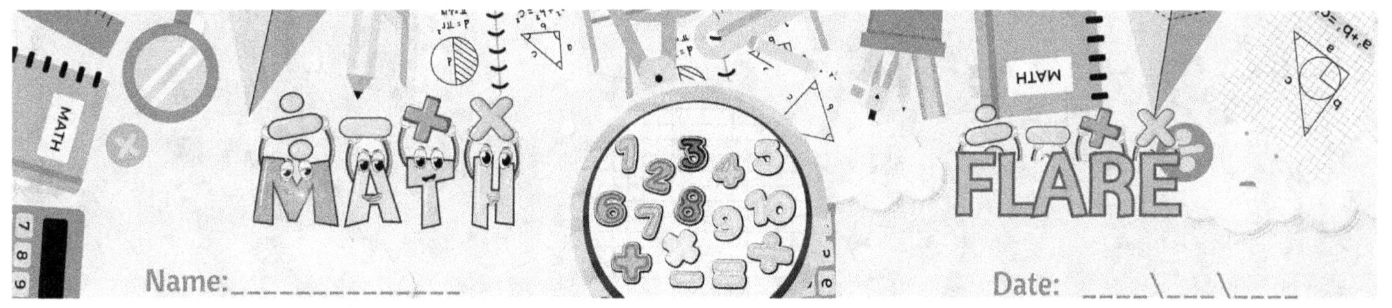

556. $\dfrac{4}{11} + \dfrac{3}{11} =$ __________

557. $\dfrac{2}{10} + \dfrac{5}{10} =$ __________

558. $\dfrac{1}{12} + \dfrac{4}{12} =$ __________

559. $\dfrac{1}{8} + \dfrac{5}{8} =$ __________

560. $\dfrac{1}{9} + \dfrac{2}{9} =$ __________

561. $\dfrac{5}{8} + \dfrac{1}{8} =$ __________

562. $\dfrac{1}{10} + \dfrac{5}{10} =$ __________

563. $\dfrac{6}{11} + \dfrac{1}{11} =$ __________

564. $\dfrac{1}{12} + \dfrac{8}{12} =$ __________

565. $\dfrac{5}{9} + \dfrac{1}{9} =$ __________

566. $\dfrac{7}{10} + \dfrac{1}{10} =$ __________

567. $\dfrac{5}{11} + \dfrac{5}{11} =$ __________

568. $\dfrac{2}{6} + \dfrac{1}{6} =$ __________

569. $\dfrac{4}{11} + \dfrac{6}{11} =$ __________

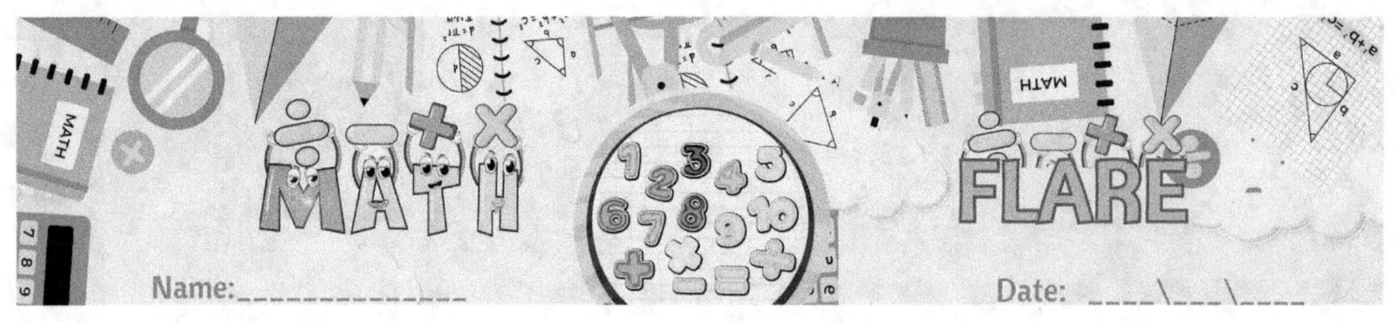

570. $\dfrac{2}{10} + \dfrac{3}{10} =$ _______________

571. $\dfrac{1}{12} + \dfrac{10}{12} =$ _______________

572. $\dfrac{2}{9} + \dfrac{4}{9} =$ _______________

573. $\dfrac{6}{10} + \dfrac{2}{10} =$ _______________

574. $\dfrac{1}{9} + \dfrac{1}{9} =$ _______________

575. $\dfrac{7}{12} + \dfrac{3}{12} =$ _______________

576. $\dfrac{4}{7} + \dfrac{1}{7} =$ _______________

577. $\dfrac{3}{9} + \dfrac{5}{9} =$ _______________

578. $\dfrac{3}{11} + \dfrac{3}{11} =$ _______________

579. $\dfrac{2}{8} + \dfrac{1}{8} =$ _______________

580. $\dfrac{4}{10} + \dfrac{4}{10} =$ _______________

581. $\dfrac{2}{12} + \dfrac{2}{12} =$ _______________

582. $\dfrac{9}{12} + \dfrac{1}{12} =$ _______________

583. $\dfrac{3}{10} + \dfrac{5}{10} =$ _______________

584. $\dfrac{4}{9} + \dfrac{1}{9} =$ ______________

585. $\dfrac{3}{11} + \dfrac{5}{11} =$ ______________

586. $\dfrac{2}{12} + \dfrac{5}{12} =$ ______________

587. $\dfrac{7}{9} + \dfrac{1}{9} =$ ______________

588. $\dfrac{4}{11} + \dfrac{4}{11} =$ ______________

589. $\dfrac{2}{11} + \dfrac{5}{11} =$ ______________

590. $\dfrac{4}{12} + \dfrac{1}{12} =$ ______________

591. $\dfrac{2}{8} + \dfrac{3}{8} =$ ______________

592. $\dfrac{1}{9} + \dfrac{7}{9} =$ ______________

593. $\dfrac{2}{11} + \dfrac{7}{11} =$ ______________

594. $\dfrac{5}{8} + \dfrac{2}{8} =$ ______________

595. $\dfrac{4}{12} + \dfrac{4}{12} =$ ______________

596. $\dfrac{4}{10} + \dfrac{2}{10} =$ ______________

597. $\dfrac{3}{11} + \dfrac{1}{11} =$ ______________

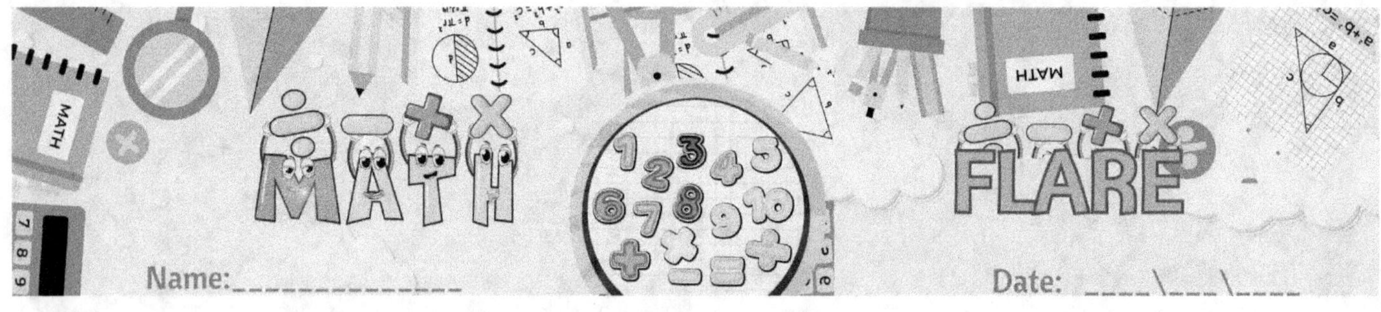

Fractions Subtraction - Common Denominator

Find the difference.

598. $\dfrac{3}{4} - \dfrac{1}{4} =$ _______________

599. $\dfrac{7}{10} - \dfrac{1}{10} =$ _______________

600. $\dfrac{3}{6} - \dfrac{2}{6} =$ _______________

601. $\dfrac{10}{12} - \dfrac{7}{12} =$ _______________

602. $\dfrac{2}{3} - \dfrac{1}{3} =$ _______________

603. $\dfrac{7}{11} - \dfrac{5}{11} =$ _______________

604. $\dfrac{9}{11} - \dfrac{7}{11} =$ _______________

605. $\dfrac{3}{4} - \dfrac{2}{4} =$ _______________

606. $\dfrac{9}{10} - \dfrac{4}{10} =$ _______________

607. $\dfrac{6}{7} - \dfrac{5}{7} =$ _______________

608. $\dfrac{4}{5} - \dfrac{1}{5} =$ _______________

609. $\dfrac{6}{8} - \dfrac{4}{8} =$ _______________

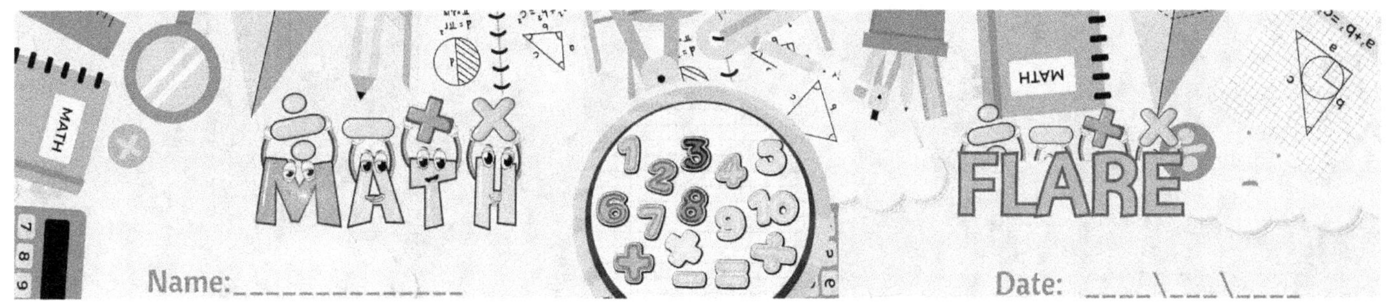

Name:_______________   Date: ______________

610. $\dfrac{8}{12} - \dfrac{5}{12} =$ _________________

611. $\dfrac{3}{9} - \dfrac{2}{9} =$ _________________

612. $\dfrac{3}{6} - \dfrac{1}{6} =$ _________________

613. $\dfrac{3}{5} - \dfrac{2}{5} =$ _________________

614. $\dfrac{7}{9} - \dfrac{5}{9} =$ _________________

615. $\dfrac{6}{10} - \dfrac{5}{10} =$ _________________

616. $\dfrac{9}{11} - \dfrac{5}{11} =$ _________________

617. $\dfrac{9}{12} - \dfrac{5}{12} =$ _________________

618. $\dfrac{5}{7} - \dfrac{2}{7} =$ _________________

619. $\dfrac{4}{8} - \dfrac{1}{8} =$ _________________

620. $\dfrac{11}{12} - \dfrac{9}{12} =$ _________________

621. $\dfrac{2}{4} - \dfrac{1}{4} =$ _________________

622. $\dfrac{10}{11} - \dfrac{1}{11} =$ _______________

623. $\dfrac{8}{10} - \dfrac{6}{10} =$ _______________

624. $\dfrac{5}{6} - \dfrac{1}{6} =$ _______________

625. $\dfrac{3}{8} - \dfrac{1}{8} =$ _______________

626. $\dfrac{8}{9} - \dfrac{7}{9} =$ _______________

627. $\dfrac{9}{12} - \dfrac{8}{12} =$ _______________

628. $\dfrac{2}{6} - \dfrac{1}{6} =$ _______________

629. $\dfrac{9}{11} - \dfrac{8}{11} =$ _______________

630. $\dfrac{7}{8} - \dfrac{4}{8} =$ _______________

631. $\dfrac{4}{5} - \dfrac{3}{5} =$ _______________

632. $\dfrac{5}{7} - \dfrac{3}{7} =$ _______________

633. $\dfrac{7}{9} - \dfrac{4}{9} =$ _______________

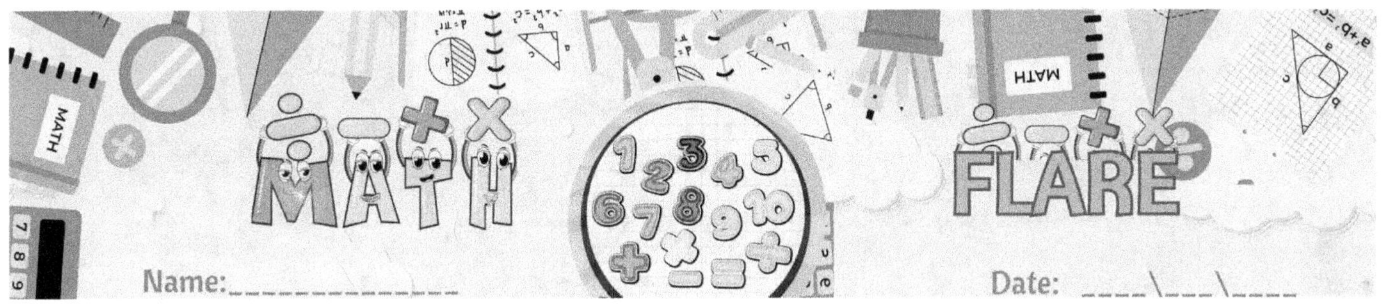

634. $\dfrac{5}{6} - \dfrac{2}{6} =$ _______________

635. $\dfrac{6}{12} - \dfrac{4}{12} =$ _______________

636. $\dfrac{6}{11} - \dfrac{1}{11} =$ _______________

637. $\dfrac{6}{8} - \dfrac{2}{8} =$ _______________

638. $\dfrac{9}{10} - \dfrac{6}{10} =$ _______________

639. $\dfrac{7}{8} - \dfrac{2}{8} =$ _______________

640. $\dfrac{4}{11} - \dfrac{2}{11} =$ _______________

641. $\dfrac{7}{12} - \dfrac{6}{12} =$ _______________

642. $\dfrac{7}{10} - \dfrac{6}{10} =$ _______________

643. $\dfrac{5}{7} - \dfrac{4}{7} =$ _______________

644. $\dfrac{6}{9} - \dfrac{5}{9} =$ _______________

645. $\dfrac{8}{12} - \dfrac{3}{12} =$ _______________

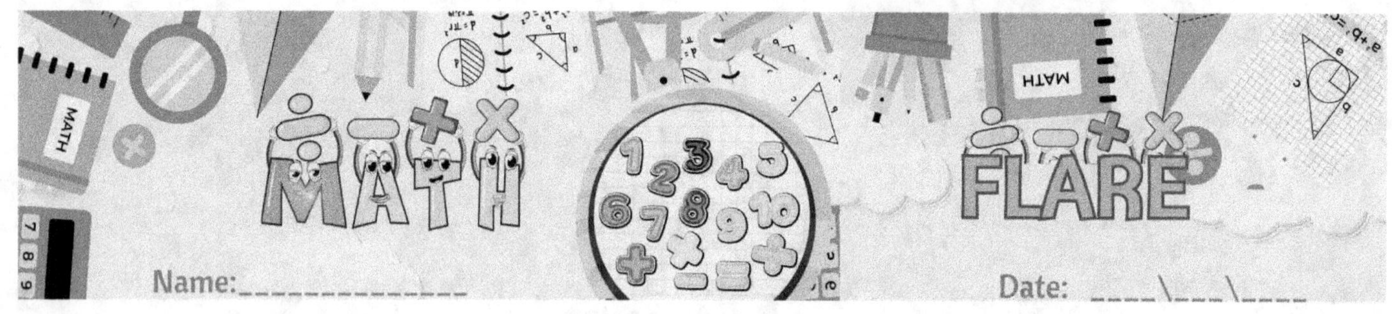

646. $\dfrac{8}{9} - \dfrac{6}{9} =$ _______________

647. $\dfrac{5}{6} - \dfrac{4}{6} =$ _______________

648. $\dfrac{10}{11} - \dfrac{4}{11} =$ _______________

649. $\dfrac{7}{10} - \dfrac{2}{10} =$ _______________

650. $\dfrac{7}{8} - \dfrac{6}{8} =$ _______________

651. $\dfrac{4}{7} - \dfrac{2}{7} =$ _______________

652. $\dfrac{2}{10} - \dfrac{1}{10} =$ _______________

653. $\dfrac{6}{7} - \dfrac{4}{7} =$ _______________

654. $\dfrac{10}{11} - \dfrac{9}{11} =$ _______________

655. $\dfrac{5}{8} - \dfrac{3}{8} =$ _______________

656. $\dfrac{3}{5} - \dfrac{1}{5} =$ _______________

657. $\dfrac{2}{9} - \dfrac{1}{9} =$ _______________

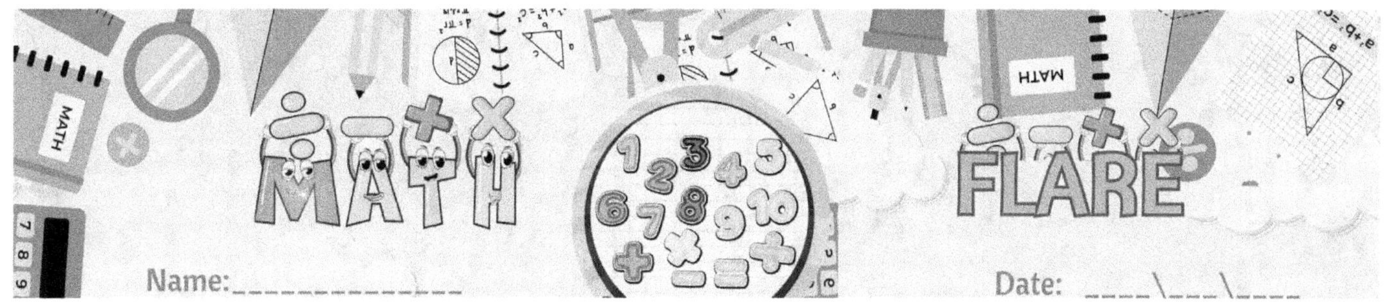

658. $\dfrac{2}{5} - \dfrac{1}{5} =$ _______________

659. $\dfrac{9}{12} - \dfrac{3}{12} =$ _______________

660. $\dfrac{3}{7} - \dfrac{2}{7} =$ _______________

661. $\dfrac{8}{11} - \dfrac{4}{11} =$ _______________

662. $\dfrac{7}{9} - \dfrac{6}{9} =$ _______________

663. $\dfrac{11}{12} - \dfrac{1}{12} =$ _______________

664. $\dfrac{9}{10} - \dfrac{7}{10} =$ _______________

665. $\dfrac{7}{8} - \dfrac{5}{8} =$ _______________

666. $\dfrac{8}{11} - \dfrac{6}{11} =$ _______________

667. $\dfrac{3}{7} - \dfrac{1}{7} =$ _______________

668. $\dfrac{8}{10} - \dfrac{5}{10} =$ _______________

669. $\dfrac{10}{12} - \dfrac{1}{12} =$ _______________

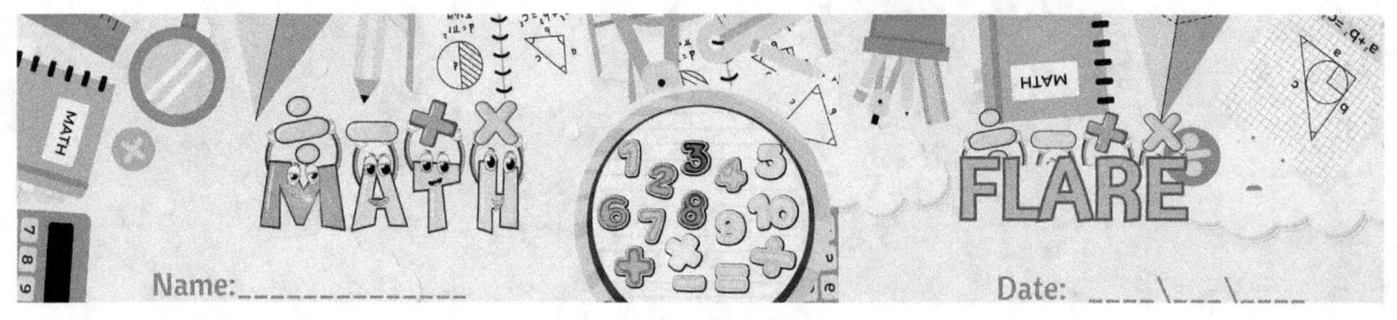

670. $\dfrac{8}{9} - \dfrac{4}{9} =$ _________________

671. $\dfrac{3}{11} - \dfrac{1}{11} =$ _________________

672. $\dfrac{5}{11} - \dfrac{1}{11} =$ _________________

673. $\dfrac{3}{10} - \dfrac{2}{10} =$ _________________

674. $\dfrac{6}{8} - \dfrac{5}{8} =$ _________________

675. $\dfrac{4}{6} - \dfrac{3}{6} =$ _________________

676. $\dfrac{11}{12} - \dfrac{5}{12} =$ _________________

677. $\dfrac{6}{12} - \dfrac{2}{12} =$ _________________

678. $\dfrac{9}{10} - \dfrac{8}{10} =$ _________________

679. $\dfrac{7}{9} - \dfrac{2}{9} =$ _________________

680. $\dfrac{6}{10} - \dfrac{2}{10} =$ _________________

681. $\dfrac{5}{8} - \dfrac{4}{8} =$ _________________

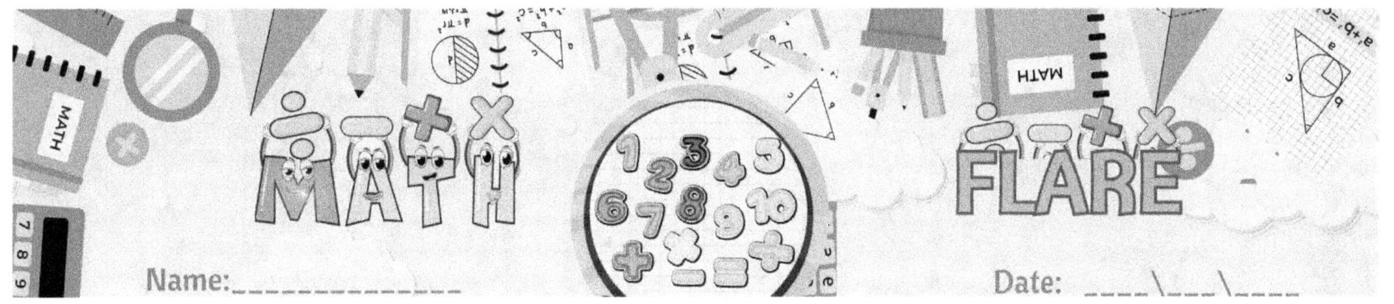

682. $\dfrac{3}{12} - \dfrac{2}{12} =$ _______________

683. $\dfrac{9}{11} - \dfrac{3}{11} =$ _______________

684. $\dfrac{6}{9} - \dfrac{1}{9} =$ _______________

685. $\dfrac{7}{11} - \dfrac{6}{11} =$ _______________

686. $\dfrac{8}{10} - \dfrac{1}{10} =$ _______________

687. $\dfrac{4}{5} - \dfrac{2}{5} =$ _______________

688. $\dfrac{6}{9} - \dfrac{3}{9} =$ _______________

689. $\dfrac{4}{6} - \dfrac{1}{6} =$ _______________

690. $\dfrac{11}{12} - \dfrac{7}{12} =$ _______________

691. $\dfrac{6}{8} - \dfrac{1}{8} =$ _______________

692. $\dfrac{6}{9} - \dfrac{4}{9} =$ _______________

693. $\dfrac{8}{11} - \dfrac{7}{11} =$ _______________

694. $\dfrac{6}{10} - \dfrac{3}{10} =$ _______________

695. $\dfrac{3}{11} - \dfrac{2}{11} =$ _______________

696. $\dfrac{4}{8} - \dfrac{2}{8} =$ _______________

697. $\dfrac{7}{12} - \dfrac{4}{12} =$ _______________

698. $\dfrac{10}{11} - \dfrac{7}{11} =$ _______________

699. $\dfrac{7}{10} - \dfrac{5}{10} =$ _______________

700. $\dfrac{10}{12} - \dfrac{5}{12} =$ _______________

701. $\dfrac{7}{9} - \dfrac{3}{9} =$ _______________

702. $\dfrac{8}{10} - \dfrac{4}{10} =$ _______________

703. $\dfrac{7}{12} - \dfrac{1}{12} =$ _______________

704. $\dfrac{8}{12} - \dfrac{7}{12} =$ _______________

705. $\dfrac{4}{7} - \dfrac{3}{7} =$ _______________

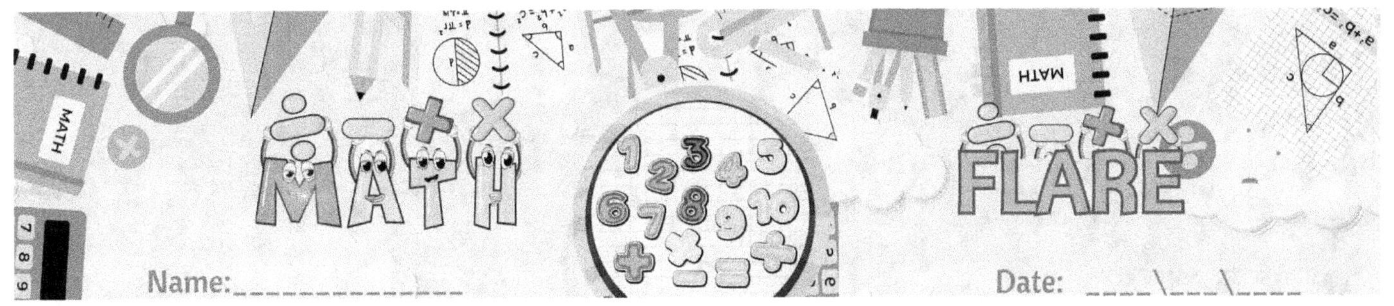

706. $\dfrac{8}{9} - \dfrac{2}{9} =$ _______________

707. $\dfrac{5}{6} - \dfrac{3}{6} =$ _______________

708. $\dfrac{10}{11} - \dfrac{6}{11} =$ _______________

709. $\dfrac{7}{8} - \dfrac{3}{8} =$ _______________

710. $\dfrac{2}{7} - \dfrac{1}{7} =$ _______________

711. $\dfrac{10}{12} - \dfrac{9}{12} =$ _______________

712. $\dfrac{10}{11} - \dfrac{8}{11} =$ _______________

713. $\dfrac{11}{12} - \dfrac{8}{12} =$ _______________

714. $\dfrac{8}{9} - \dfrac{5}{9} =$ _______________

715. $\dfrac{4}{10} - \dfrac{2}{10} =$ _______________

716. $\dfrac{6}{7} - \dfrac{1}{7} =$ _______________

717. $\dfrac{9}{11} - \dfrac{6}{11} =$ _______________

718. $\dfrac{11}{12} - \dfrac{4}{12} =$ _______________

719. $\dfrac{4}{9} - \dfrac{3}{9} =$ _______________

720. $\dfrac{9}{12} - \dfrac{4}{12} =$ _______________

721. $\dfrac{6}{9} - \dfrac{2}{9} =$ _______________

722. $\dfrac{5}{12} - \dfrac{3}{12} =$ _______________

723. $\dfrac{6}{11} - \dfrac{5}{11} =$ _______________

724. $\dfrac{8}{12} - \dfrac{1}{12} =$ _______________

725. $\dfrac{8}{10} - \dfrac{3}{10} =$ _______________

726. $\dfrac{9}{12} - \dfrac{7}{12} =$ _______________

727. $\dfrac{2}{11} - \dfrac{1}{11} =$ _______________

728. $\dfrac{7}{12} - \dfrac{5}{12} =$ _______________

729. $\dfrac{5}{11} - \dfrac{2}{11} =$ _______________

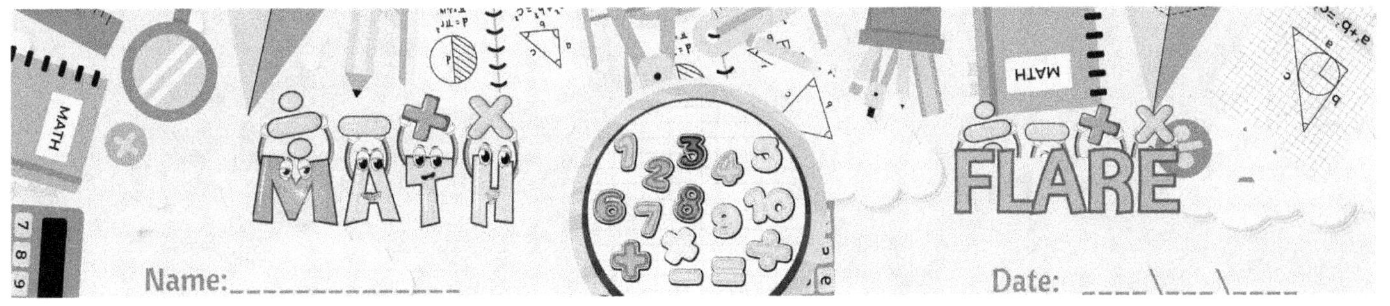

Name:________________   Date: _______________

730. $\dfrac{8}{10} - \dfrac{7}{10} =$ _______________

731. $\dfrac{2}{8} - \dfrac{1}{8} =$ _______________

732. $\dfrac{10}{12} - \dfrac{3}{12} =$ _______________

733. $\dfrac{5}{9} - \dfrac{4}{9} =$ _______________

734. $\dfrac{5}{9} - \dfrac{1}{9} =$ _______________

735. $\dfrac{6}{10} - \dfrac{1}{10} =$ _______________

736. $\dfrac{10}{11} - \dfrac{5}{11} =$ _______________

737. $\dfrac{7}{11} - \dfrac{3}{11} =$ _______________

738. $\dfrac{3}{10} - \dfrac{1}{10} =$ _______________

739. $\dfrac{6}{7} - \dfrac{3}{7} =$ _______________

740. $\dfrac{3}{12} - \dfrac{1}{12} =$ _______________

741. $\dfrac{7}{10} - \dfrac{4}{10} =$ _______________

ANSWERS

Page 1: Adding Decimals

1. 169.07	2. 114.44	3. 186.26	4. 182.39	5. 140.82
6. 79.96	7. 37.58	8. 102.54	9. 162.93	10. 94.24
11. 31.81	12. 117.79	13. 85.06	14. 76.65	15. 124.82
16. 114.28	17. 69.00	18. 59.58	19. 69.21	20. 123.37
21. 163.63	22. 97.21	23. 149.73	24. 150.56	25. 101.41
26. 30.45	27. 147.61	28. 188.18	29. 89.31	30. 128.69
31. 127.19	32. 137.04	33. 110.94	34. 107.40	35. 175.21
36. 105.31	37. 48.21	38. 87.17	39. 140.58	40. 85.59
41. 146.15	42. 170.89	43. 90.31	44. 108.31	45. 56.39
46. 95.00	47. 79.49	48. 39.59	49. 83.23	50. 131.89
51. 143.70	52. 159.34	53. 70.02	54. 177.50	55. 76.81
56. 120.67	57. 33.51	58. 163.36	59. 159.17	60. 79.74
61. 135.70	62. 156.59	63. 63.20	64. 115.25	65. 37.88
66. 58.27	67. 163.04	68. 110.22	69. 92.72	70. 119.45
71. 41.03	72. 158.19	73. 97.62	74. 66.58	75. 70.46
76. 94.36	77. 87.40	78. 190.00	79. 110.95	80. 119.99
81. 140.42	82. 92.27	83. 48.40	84. 51.31	85. 94.51
86. 112.37	87. 158.09	88. 91.37	89. 134.18	90. 99.28
91. 88.63	92. 163.91	93. 159.24	94. 126.02	95. 169.85

96. 97.63   97. 107.69   98. 114.18   99. 125.88   100. 141.30

Page 6: Subtracting Decimals

101. 23.63   102. 36.38   103. 25.71   104. 12.67   105. 45.38

106. 12.50   107. 30.23   108. 11.63   109. 38.95   110. 12.75

111. 65.37   112. 1.86   113. 34.17   114. 34.17   115. 30.20

116. 42.48   117. 53.88   118. 47.60   119. 5.52   120. 12.47

121. 3.02   122. 34.72   123. 42.62   124. 39.41   125. 13.33

126. 5.79   127. 8.24   128. 35.49   129. 24.64   130. 28.53

131. 39.34   132. 18.58   133. 36.29   134. 21.64   135. 33.03

136. 2.85   137. 12.06   138. 55.23   139. 43.10   140. 5.58

141. 25.52   142. 51.65   143. 47.92   144. 23.36   145. 45.04

146. 15.10   147. 49.07   148. 40.64   149. 59.76   150. 47.90

151. 9.01   152. 15.91   153. 4.11   154. 20.21   155. 8.63

156. 78.80   157. 37.41   158. 0.31   159. 37.07   160. 56.75

161. 74.83   162. 61.58   163. 69.42   164. 58.50   165. 36.36

166. 25.37   167. 83.61   168. 51.61   169. 18.16   170. 38.27

171. 32.52   172. 22.08   173. 58.77   174. 28.26   175. 41.12

176. 43.40   177. 20.90   178. 15.66   179. 34.49   180. 11.25

181. 40.45   182. 29.31   183. 25.13   184. 73.59   185. 3.08

186. 13.56   187. 9.33   188. 7.37   189. 39.90   190. 71.69

191. 41.92   192. 1.72   193. 45.94   194. 3.65   195. 7.20

196. 0.52   197. 36.98   198. 11.39   199. 17.14   200. 54.52

Page 11: Fraction Identification

201. 1/16   202. 1/2   203. 1/2   204. 1/2   205. 7/15   206. 2/3

207. 1/2   208. 2/5   209. 2/3   210. 6/7   211. 1/9   212. 2/15

213. 1/6   214. 3/8   215. 3/10   216. 1/4   217. 5/7   218. 4/5

219. 11/16   220. 1/3   221. 3/5   222. 1/6   223. 1/10   224. 3/4

225. 2/9   226. 2/7   227. 3/5   228. 1/3   229. 1/4   230. 3/7

231. 11/12   232. 4/5   233. 7/16   234. 7/9   235. 2/3   236. 5/6

237. 1/4   238. 5/6   239. 4/9   240. 2/3   241. 5/9   242. 1/3

243. 1/5   244. 4/7   245. 15/16   246. 7/12   247. 1/8   248. 1/3

249. 8/9   250. 9/16   251. 2/5   252. 1/7   253. 1/2   254. 7/8

255. 11/15   256. 2/5   257. 2/3   258. 1/8   259. 1/15   260. 1/2

261. 13/16   262. 5/12   263. 3/8   264. 9/10   265. 3/4   266. 3/4

267. 7/10   268. 1/3   269. 4/5   270. 7/8   271. 14/15   272. 1/4

273. 8/15   274. 5/16   275. 5/8   276. 3/4   277. 5/8   278. 3/16

279. 3/5   280. 1/5   281. 1/12   282. 4/15   283. 1/5   284. 13/15

285. 1/2   286. 5/8   287. 1/2   288. 4/5   289. 6/7   290. 5/8

291. 4/5   292. 1/2   293. 1/7   294. 1/6   295. 4/7

Page 23: Compare the Fractions

296. <   297. >   298. <   299. <   300. >   301. >   302. >   303. <

304. >   305. >   306. >   307. <   308. >   309. >   310. <   311. >

312. >   313. <   314. >   315. >   316. >   317. >   318. <   319. =

320. >   321. >   322. <   323. >   324. <   325. >   326. >   327. >

328. >   329. <   330. >   331. <   332. <   333. >   334. >   335. <

336. <   337. >   338. <   339. >   340. <   341. <   342. <   343. >

344. >   345. =   346. <   347. >   348. >   349. <   350. <   351. =

352. <   353. >   354. <   355. >   356. >   357. >   358. <   359. <

360. <   361. >   362. >   363. <   364. <   365. >   366. >   367. >

368. >   369. <   370. <   371. >   372. <   373. <   374. <   375. >

376. <   377. <   378. >   379. >   380. <   381. <   382. <   383. <

384. <   385. <   386. >   387. <   388. >   389. <   390. <   391. <

392. <   393. >   394. <   395. =   396. =   397. >   398. =   399. <

400. <   401. >

Page 32: Equivalent Fractions

402. 112   403. 9   404. 2   405. 12   406. 5   407. 12   408. 9

409. 10   410. 24   411. 18   412. 35   413. 10   414. 4   415. 7

416. 120   417. 10   418. 52   419. 7   420. 126   421. 140   422. 6

423. 1   424. 32   425. 3   426. 14   427. 5   428. 11   429. 8

430. 20   431. 3   432. 153   433. 4   434. 18   435. 8   436. 3

437. 6   438. 16   439. 56   440. 2   441. 4   442. 17   443. 152

444. 1   445. 36   446. 9   447. 2   448. 15   449. 20   450. 144

451. 1   452. 2   453. 4   454. 3   455. 2   456. 5   457. 9

458. 36   459. 9

Page 37:   Fractions Addition: Common Denominator

460. 11/12   461. 2/3   462. 2/3   463. 7/9   464. 5/6   465. 7/8

466. 1/1   467. 2/5   468. 4/5   469. 3/4   470. 4/7   471. 10/11

472. 2/3   473. 6/11   474. 7/9   475. 7/10   476. 5/8   477. 4/5

478. 1/2   479. 3/4   480. 6/7   481. 5/6   482. 5/9   483. 7/10

484. 7/8   485. 1/2   486. 8/11   487. 6/7   488. 1/4   489. 7/10

490. 1/2   491. 8/9   492. 1/2   493. 4/7   494. 10/11   495. 2/7

496. 5/6   497. 10/11   498. 1/4   499. 7/9   500. 3/8   501. 2/5

502. 9/11   503. 3/4   504. 2/5   505. 11/12   506. 3/5   507. 8/9

508. 5/6   509. 5/6   510. 9/10   511. 5/7   512. 7/9   513. 4/11

514. 9/10   515. 4/9   516. 4/5   517. 3/11   518. 5/12   519. 5/7

520. 7/9   521. 2/3   522. 4/5   523. 7/8   524. 7/10   525. 4/11

526. 6/7   527. 2/3   528. 4/9   529. 3/4   530. 2/3   531. 5/11

532. 1/2   533. 5/6   534. 4/5   535. 3/5   536. 3/4   537. 8/11

538. 7/8   539. 11/12   540. 8/11   541. 9/10   542. 1/3   543. 7/9

544. 7/8   545. 7/11   546. 6/7   547. 3/4   548. 3/5   549. 5/12

550. 3/4   551. 1/2   552. 5/9   553. 5/6   554. 8/11   555. 2/3

556. 7/11   557. 7/10   558. 5/12   559. 3/4   560. 1/3   561. 3/4

562. 3/5   563. 7/11   564. 3/4   565. 2/3   566. 4/5   567. 10/11

568. 1/2   569. 10/11   570. 1/2   571. 11/12   572. 2/3   573. 4/5

574. 2/9   575. 5/6   576. 5/7   577. 8/9   578. 6/11   579. 3/8

580. 4/5   581. 1/3   582. 5/6   583. 4/5   584. 5/9   585. 8/11

586. 7/12   587. 8/9   588. 8/11   589. 7/11   590. 5/12   591. 5/8

592. 8/9   593. 9/11   594. 7/8   595. 2/3   596. 3/5   597. 4/11

Page 47: Fractions Subtraction - Common Denominator

598. 1/2   599. 3/5   600. 1/6   601. 1/4   602. 1/3   603. 2/11

604. 2/11   605. 1/4   606. 1/2   607. 1/7   608. 3/5   609. 1/4

610. 1/4   611. 1/9   612. 1/3   613. 1/5   614. 2/9   615. 1/10

616. 4/11   617. 1/3   618. 3/7   619. 3/8   620. 1/6   621. 1/4

622. 9/11   623. 1/5   624. 2/3   625. 1/4   626. 1/9   627. 1/12

628. 1/6   629. 1/11   630. 3/8   631. 1/5   632. 2/7   633. 1/3

634. 1/2   635. 1/6   636. 5/11   637. 1/2   638. 3/10   639. 5/8

640. 2/11   641. 1/12   642. 1/10   643. 1/7   644. 1/9   645. 5/12

646. 2/9   647. 1/6   648. 6/11   649. 1/2   650. 1/8   651. 2/7

652. 1/10   653. 2/7   654. 1/11   655. 1/4   656. 2/5   657. 1/9

658. 1/5   659. 1/2   660. 1/7   661. 4/11   662. 1/9   663. 5/6

664. 1/5   665. 1/4   666. 2/11   667. 2/7   668. 3/10   669. 3/4

670. 4/9   671. 2/11   672. 4/11   673. 1/10   674. 1/8   675. 1/6

676. 1/2   677. 1/3   678. 1/10   679. 5/9   680. 2/5   681. 1/8

682. 1/12   683. 6/11   684. 5/9   685. 1/11   686. 7/10   687. 2/5

688. 1/3   689. 1/2   690. 1/3   691. 5/8   692. 2/9   693. 1/11

694. 3/10   695. 1/11   696. 1/4   697. 1/4   698. 3/11   699. 1/5

700. 5/12   701. 4/9   702. 2/5   703. 1/2   704. 1/12   705. 1/7

706. 2/3   707. 1/3   708. 4/11   709. 1/2   710. 1/7   711. 1/12

712. 2/11   713. 1/4   714. 1/3   715. 1/5   716. 5/7   717. 3/11

718. 7/12   719. 1/9   720. 5/12   721. 4/9   722. 1/6   723. 1/11

724. 7/12   725. 1/2   726. 1/6   727. 1/11   728. 1/6   729. 3/11

730. 1/10   731. 1/8   732. 7/12   733. 1/9   734. 4/9   735. 1/2

736. 5/11   737. 4/11   738. 1/5   739. 3/7   740. 1/6   741. 3/10